Across the Savage Sea

Across the
Savage Sea

THE FIRST WOMAN
TO ROW ACROSS THE NORTH ATLANTIC

MAUD FONTENOY

Foreword by Gérard d'Aboville
Translated from the French by Martin Sokolinsky

Arcade Publishing • New York

FIRST ENGLISH–LANGUAGE EDITION

First published in France as *Atlantique Face Nord* by Editions Robert
Laffont

Library of Congress Cataloging-in-Publication Data

Fontenoy, Maud.
   [Atlantique face nord. English]
   Across the savage sea : the first woman to row across the North
Atlantic / by Maud Fontenoy ; foreword by Gérard d'Aboville ; translated
from the French by Martin Sokolinsky. — 1st English-language ed.
    p. cm.
  ISBN 1-55970-762-3
  1. Fontenoy, Maud. 2. Rowers — France — Biography. 3. Boats and
boating — North Atlantic Ocean. I. Title.

GV790.92.F66A3 2005
797.12'3'092 — dc22   2004023459

Published in the United States by Arcade Publishing, Inc., New York
Distributed by Time Warner Book Group

Visit our Web site at www.arcadepub.com
Visit the author's Web site at www.maudfontenoy.com

10 9 8 7 6 5 4 3 2 1

Designed by API

EB

PRINTED IN THE UNITED STATES OF AMERICA

To Marc, my guardian angel

To follow the dream, and again
to follow the dream — and so — always —
usque ad finem . . .

— Joseph Conrad, *Lord Jim*

Contents

Foreword

I WANT TO ROW ACROSS THE ATLANTIC ALONE."
The plan took my breath away.* She wanted to cross the
immensity of the ocean in a tiny boat, using a pair of oars as
her sole means of propulsion. Such a feat would depend
entirely on her will, her tenacity. She would need the courage
of Guillaumet, the French aviator, who crashed in the Andes
and lived to tell about it. He summed up his battle for survival
in this sentence: "No animal on earth would have endured
what I went through."

Yet when Maud Fontenoy, my goddaughter, announced
her plan to me, she wasn't telling the half of it. A point insignificant to the layman but vitally important to the mariner
was the direction in which she meant to cross.

The North Atlantic can be crossed either by the
southerly route — that is, leaving, say, the Canary Islands, and
heading for the West Indies — or by the northerly route, starting
from the eastern seaboard of North America and sailing to
the coast of Europe.

The American Tori Murden, who had tried this
northerly crossing in the summer of 1999 and been forced to
quit after several terrifying capsizes, later succeeded in crossing by the southerly route, leaving from the Canaries. On her

---

*A sentiment that was understandable since Gérard d'Aboville rowed across both
the Atlantic, and later across the Pacific Ocean. He knew whereof he spoke.

arrival in Guadeloupe, she said: "The highest wave that I encountered on this trip wasn't as high as the smallest wave I ran into up north." No doubt this is something of an exaggeration but it does sum up the situation fairly well.

On the southerly track, you can expect a pleasant climate, dominated by trade winds that almost never reach gale force and, most important, blow in the right direction, guaranteeing steady progress.

On the northerly track, in contrast, crossing from America to Europe, the climatic data are totally different. One might describe it as another world. There, the ocean is dominated by depressions that generate storms, with winds veering from south to west and then the northwest, creating cross-currents highly dangerous for small craft. Some of these depressions, former tropical hurricanes, can come sweeping across the Atlantic, creating nightmarish conditions. Aside from these depressions — that is, during periods of good weather — it often happens that the winds blow from the east or northeast, thus making any headway impossible.

Up to this time, only six rowers — all men — had managed to make this crossing.

"All right, Maud, which way do you plan to cross?"

"By the northerly route, of course. I want to be the first woman to do it."

I spent a long time explaining the dangers of such an undertaking. On this track, many ill-fated attempts had ended with the rowers asking to be taken off, with the boats going down and, in six cases, with death.

Maud understood. She knew the sea and its hazards, but

despite my warnings, she stuck to her plan. I gave her still further warnings:

"You plan to sail this coming summer. In a few months you've got to find a yard, have the boat built, put together all your gear, and then ship the whole kit and caboodle to the other side of the Atlantic. That's going to cost you an arm and a leg. Do you have any backers?"

"No, I'm going to look for them. But it's not all that important. I work — I'll take a loan, and if necessary I'll finance the expedition myself."

I had to hand it to her for determination. She was going to row and I felt she could make it. I decided to help her.

If I had tried to paint a grim picture, I still would have been nowhere near the reality. While the French remember the summer of 2003 for its heat wave, it must be recalled that, in the North Atlantic, such exceptionally warm weather was translated into long periods of wind from the east. Imagine Maud's despair at losing, in 24 hours, all the ground she had gained in a week of bitter struggle. Imagine her anguish at seeing her crossing take longer than her worst-case scenarios, with more and more frequent gales, days getting shorter, food and water running low, her landfall increasingly uncertain. . . .

The North Atlantic spared her nothing. True, the uncertainties of the weather form an integral part of the risks of such a voyage, but her sliding seat was torn off by a breaking sea and, even worse, the two desalinators malfunctioned. Anyone else would have thrown in the towel.

Opening this book, you will set out on a bad journey.

With Maud, you learn what it is to be sodden and cold off Newfoundland, to feel the dread of being run down by large vessels, and the horror of gale-tossed nights. There, wedged into a tiny cabin, like a prisoner, her limbs swollen, nerves shattered, Maud awaits the final capsize, the rogue sea that will splinter her boat into matchsticks. You will share her pathetic attempts at escape, her rare moments of happiness, communing with nature in the calm after a storm, her hopes for a different life, and a future that will enable her to stand an unbearable present.

"But why do it?" the skeptics asked. "Why put yourself in such a predicament? What's the point of it?"

"There is no point," I once replied to this question, but made sure to add: "It's like Mozart — it serves no purpose."

If we eliminated everything that was "useless," what would be left? With all artistic expression gone, we would wear only gray because it doesn't show the dirt, and drink nothing but water since it's all we need to slake our thirst. Our relationships would be limited to what is essential and practical. Just try to imagine it. The engineer Eiffel designed many extremely useful bridges and tunnels. He is remembered only for the Eiffel Tower, that monument of uselessness. But how it expresses our dreams!

Of all the creatures on earth, Man is the only one whose actions are not guided solely by instinct — but also survival and reproduction. I think this faculty was given to us because we possess exactly that dimension lacking in animals: our dreams and the power to imagine other places, just as Maud continued to imagine her landfall.

Thank you, Maud, for having made us dream, for having transformed the impossible into the possible. Because it is our need to test ourselves and push the envelope, our fascination with exceeding our limits, which is not only the key to our progress, but also our reason for being, our reason for hoping.

— Gérard d'Aboville

THE ROUTE

Departure from Saint-Pierre and Miquelon (French territory off Canada) on June 13, 2003.
Arrival at La Coruña, Spain, on October 9, 2003.

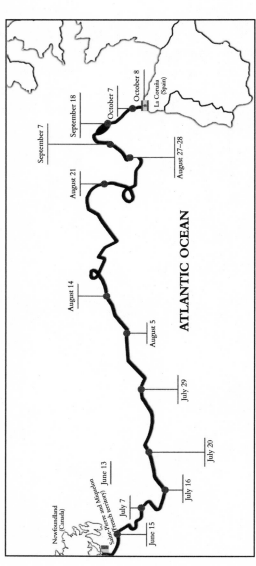

June 15: First gale and first capsize • July 7: Icebergs and fog • July 16: Whale sightings — arrival in the Gulf Stream
July 20: Tropical storm Dany — wave height fifteen to eighteen feet; wind forty knots • July 29: *Pilot* narrowly misses colliding
with container ship • August 5: Halfway • August 14: Porpoise and dolphin sightings • August 21: First desalinator breaks down
August 27–28 Terrible storm — wave height thirty feet and wind fifty knots — seventeen capsizings in one night
September 7: Maud's birthday — two capsizings • September 18: Reserve desalinator breaks down — Maud drinks seawater
October 7: Dreadful fright as trawler nearly runs down *Pilot.*

Graphics: Thomas Bez / Jean-Christophe L'Espagnol

Part One

The White Hell of
the Grand Banks of
Newfoundland

1

First Storm — Memories of Saint-Pierre — First Days at Sea

*K*EEP YOUR CHIN UP. Whatever it takes, you have to hang in there. You've got to make it."

Scrunched up in the tiny aft cabin, I was so sick and exhausted I couldn't keep my head from lolling against the bulkheads. *Pilot,* my boat, lay broadside to the troughs, rolling violently, buried continuously under twelve- to fifteen-foot waves.

My stomach felt like it had been turned inside out. I was seasick, drenched, frozen, crying in pain and panic. I just wanted to hide somewhere, to vanish.

I begged in a rasping, cracking voice: "Please, won't somebody get me out of this prison? I can't take this anymore. Just don't break up on me now, *Pilot.* You hang in there for me, okay?"

With thunderous crashes, the sea smacked against the boat's belly harder and harder. Every time *Pilot*'s hull came crashing down in a trough, my whole body shook violently. I had a migraine headache because there wasn't enough air to breathe. The aft cabin, measuring about three feet high by three feet wide, soon became a dank, suffocating cage. In that claustrophobic space, a candle died in less than ten minutes. My temples felt as if they were caught in the jaws of a vise. Trembling with fear, I curled into a fetal position. I used my eiderdown quilt to absorb the pounding, wedging myself in so that I wouldn't be flung against the planking of the hull. I just wanted it to stop.

Taking a sickening elevator ride, *Pilot* plunged from wave crests to troughs. I could almost hear her sobbing. It wasn't supposed to be happening like this. No, not this bad, not right from the start! I could never stand three months of this kind of weather. Pitching and plunging wildly, *Pilot* groaned as the seas smacked into the half-inch planks of her hull. Massive waves tossed us around like some kind of pathetic toy, savagely shaking us, hurling us violently in every direction. There was no way of telling where the next assault would come from. This had been going on for five hours now, and I still couldn't breathe. I had a bucket in one hand, ready for the next round of seasickness. The other held the hatch, hoping to crack it enough to let in a bit of air. But the North Atlantic gave us no respite. Disaster struck the next second. A huge breaking wave crashed into our port side, and *Pilot* rolled over onto her beam-ends before I could reach for the grab-rail. My head caromed off the Plexiglas observation bubble in the cabin roof, leaving me stunned. Icy water came flooding through the partially open hatch, I saw my foul-weather jacket awash in a mixture of seawater and vomit. *Pilot*'s luck seemed to have run out. It was my first capsize.

*   *   *

I had to react fast. There was only one thing on my mind: surviving. I lunged for the Plexiglas hatch and pulled it shut. I had no intention of letting my boat sink. Poor little *Pilot* had turned upside down. I couldn't keep myself steady — I went over with her. It felt like the end of the world. Everything went black. In terror, I shut my eyes and clung to the grab-rail that had been installed alongside my bunk. I stayed that way for a few seconds. I couldn't see anything, but I knew the galley stove was directly over my head. There must have been some water left in the kettle because it was streaming down onto my hair. Then a new wave set us upright again. I fell back on my bunk, dazed, unable to understand what had just happened. I had to grit my teeth as pain shot through my wrist. I prayed that it wasn't broken.

"I can't take this anymore. I just don't want to die out here, not like this . . ."

I started crying again. But this time, I couldn't stop. I hurt everywhere. I was in a state of shock. The cabin stank to high heaven, and there I was — shivering, cold, the right side of my face sore and swollen after hitting the cabin roof. I felt like an animal, an exhausted, filthy animal thrown back into a cage after being forced to fight. Utterly wiped out, I sat there, rocking back and forth, struggling to regain my composure. I had the urge to throw myself into someone's arms, to cry on someone's shoulder. I would have given anything to sleep, to forget everything and wake up somewhere else. Pretending that I wasn't all alone, I invented another person who could help me get through my anguish, my distress, in the blackness of that night in which *Pilot* and I were imprisoned.

Without realizing it, I began stroking my hair, and it was as if the hand of another were caressing me.

I was unable to move for hours, trying to get over my fright. I did my best to cheer up, to smile. I kept telling myself that everything was all right, that the situation wasn't so bad, that I was still me. It was just my body that had taken a beating — not my spirit. Someday I would forget these moments of anguish.

This was only my first gale. But it was a lot worse than I had anticipated. And I knew I was going to run into a lot more of them.

The gale had come up suddenly. The drogue I set out hadn't held for long. This sea anchor, capable of holding *Pilot's* bow into the wind and waves, was a small parachute canopy; its rope, a long nylon line three-eighths of an inch (10mm) in diameter, was rated to lift three times the weight of my boat. But the sudden pulls exerted on such a drogue in a gale are enormous. The line snapped after only an hour and we lost it — unfortunately, it was the largest anchor I had. The North Atlantic route meant days of adverse winds, so the drogue was vital in slowing my drift. My crossing having just begun, I had no way of knowing just how badly I would miss that drogue.

I couldn't help kicking myself. I should have realized how much stress the wind could put on the line. I should never have heaved that sea anchor. I could have set out the smaller one so as to reduce the strain. True, the gale had been forecast, but the winds weren't supposed to exceed 20–25 knots — just enough to toss the boat around a bit. I knew I could handle that — it was a situation I was ready for. And besides, I'd already made the decision to set out. But just two days after my departure, the wind began to rise. The ocean turned a nasty gray and the waves began to tumble in ranks fifteen feet high. I hadn't found my sea legs at all. I had neither accustomed myself to my new living space nor to *Pilot*'s totally chaotic, totally unpredictable pitching and rolling. There I was, helpless, watching the weather turn into a gale.

Battered, disoriented, I couldn't relax. In forty-eight hours, I hadn't slept a minute. I'd been too seasick to eat a thing. It was mid-June, yet icebergs surrounded me. They loomed over my little boat like cliffs and, in darkness or poor visibility, I couldn't see them coming. I was on the Grand Banks of Newfoundland, those dangerous shoals that make the waves short, choppy, confused. The shallow, sandy banks lying only a hundred or so feet beneath my boat made the sea capricious and violent.

The fog became increasingly dense. We were enveloped in it and, abruptly, the visibility dropped to less than three yards.

"Don't be afraid, *Pilot*," I whispered. The storm had begun.

Isolated on my tiny boat, lost on the expanse of the ocean, I thought about my last few days on dry land. It brought a tear to my eye remembering Saint-Pierre and Miquelon, the islanders' friendliness and generosity.

The day I arrived on the island, the rough hands of fifteen dockworkers eased *Pilot* out of her freight container as gently as if they were removing a jewel from its case. I watched them work: they were utterly astonished at what they saw. I told them my little story. They were simply baffled — why on earth would anyone want to put to sea in something as flimsy as that?

"No, you're joking. Her?"

"No, it's no joke. The girl over there — the one talking to Jean-Louis Bernardelli, the sports journalist — that's the girl rower."

A tall, thickset man pointed at me. "*That little blonde?* That can't be!"

These men — fishermen used to the North Atlantic cold — knew the sea all too well. The sea had taught them about suffering, weathered their faces, hardened their resolve. It had taken their grandfathers, their fathers, and, for some, it had taken their sons. They knew that the sea was unrelenting, cruel, and unpredictable. Most of all, they knew it was no place for a woman. They understood the dangers of that rocky coast where the fog never lifted. They'd grown up hearing tales of their ancestors fishing for cod from their dories. They'd heard about schooners vanishing in the fog, about crews that were lost and never came back.

I stood there among the fishermen, somewhat daunted. Their astonished gaze left me uncomfortable. I had decided to set out from Saint-Pierre after meeting islanders at the Paris Boat Show. I had been charmed by their warmth and enthusiasm, their offers of assistance; and the fact that this island off Newfoundland belonged to France had been the clincher. Now, standing there in front of them, I tried to look confident even though I was shaking in my boots. Deep down was a gnawing doubt, fear that I wouldn't make it, that I hadn't properly gauged the danger, that I was unprepared.

Yet, I had done my homework. I'd thought out each step very carefully, considered every piece of advice, weighed all the problems and found solutions for each of them before setting out. I had made list upon list of things not to forget, things to check. I'd left nothing to chance. On a trip like this, either you made your own luck or you didn't come back.

I had also spent many hours getting in shape. In addition to thousands of push-ups and crunches, I'd forced myself into a daily regimen of running. I'd picked running because it was something I really despised. To tell the truth, there had been plenty of times when I'd even had to force myself to row. But I was excited — I'd thought about the transatlantic crossing day and night. Throughout those long months, I'd force myself to imagine how it would be when the chips were down. I meant to convince myself that it was all a matter of willpower, that nothing could make me give up and that *this* really was my dream. You just had to start out properly motivated, with your thinking clear. I had made up my mind that I was going all the way. But I hadn't even left Saint-Pierre and I was already trembling. I knew I couldn't afford to put off my starting date.

The first man to solo the Pacific under oars, Gérard d'Aboville, had told me again and again: "Maud, the only thing you'll be able to choose is the weather on the day you sail."

Temperatures had been very low that year, and even now, in midsummer, the icebergs still hadn't melted. Hundreds of enormous bergs had grounded on sandbars — especially on the Grand Banks off Newfoundland's southeast coast. Invisible in the fog, these mountains of ice lay in wait for me. Like the freighters that plied these waters, I would have to go around the bergs, circling them to the south. And this meant adding many extra miles to my voyage. As for the wind, I had gradually come to accept that I couldn't hope for more than two days of fair winds. Each morning, I walked down to the French National Meteorological Bureau and entered hesitantly, fearful of having them inform me about a storm. I sensed their discomfort. They avoided my eyes, not daring to tell me what they really thought of my plan. They were afraid — afraid of being held responsible for allowing me to go. They nevertheless did their best to help me with my preparations. The closer the departure date came, the more they pampered me, as if I were setting off on a voyage from which I would never return. I had the strangely disturbing feeling that I was a prisoner on death row. I sensed my new friends' apprehension at seeing me put to sea. They all had hoped I would give up and now were saddened to see how stubborn I was.

"It's such a pity — she's so nice," one elderly woman said to another, just within earshot.

Curious onlookers walked out on the float — to snap my picture, give me a kiss, and offer a word of encouragement.

"So that's it, eh? You're really going through with it?"

And I was. I'd already begun my countdown. The predicted gale was badly timed, but I knew I had to get out of Saint-Pierre once and for all. Postponing the start once more wouldn't help matters a bit. The weather reports had been dismal for more than three weeks already. Though far from ideal, these conditions might be the best for a long time. Time had rushed by since my arrival on the island a few weeks before, and the waiting had become unbearable. The longer I put off setting out, the later in the year I would reach the other side. There as well, off the European continent, the risks would be greater the later into the autumn we arrived. Should I start? Should I keep on waiting? That morning I took the plunge. Taking a deep breath, I told everybody that I was starting out the very next day. On top of everything else, it would be Friday — the 13th. A few people shook their heads, but I tried to forget about that superstition and pretended not to understand the astonishment of the Saint-Pierre fishermen. I concentrated on all the things that I still had to prepare. This was definitely not the time to forget any pieces of equipment. Not when you're undertaking a trip like this.

"Nobody's going to bring you a toothbrush or shampoo when you're all the way out there," my mother, Chantal, had joked.

I really started getting nervous. For a week now, I'd been alone in Saint-Pierre, as both my father, Marc, and the naval architect who'd designed my boat, Marc Ginesty, had flown back to Paris. It felt odd being there by myself. I suddenly felt the weight on my shoulders: now I had to take over; the burden of responsibility was mine and mine alone. But wasn't that exactly what I'd always wanted? Yes, definitely, I was up for this ride.

"*Don't go!* All you have to do is say, 'April Fool!' Tell them it was just a gag," Marc told me at the airport before hugging me.

There was no way. In spite of my anxiety, I couldn't wait to get started.

I felt immense pressure, but also tremendous enthusiasm, excitement at knowing that soon I would only be able to count on myself. Right up to the last minute, I constantly expected some unforeseen mishap, some ridiculous glitch to prevent me from setting out. After all that anticipation, I kept my fingers crossed that I wouldn't break a leg or get sick on the eve of the trip.

That last morning on dry land, I busied myself in the cabin securing two small hammocks made of netting. They would hold the fresh fruit I was taking along. Just then a fisherman stepped aboard. He wanted to give me a Saint Christopher medal. And not just any medal, but his medal, the one from his boat, the medal that had protected him throughout a lifetime of fishing on the Grand Banks. He placed it in the palm of my hand and then, visibly upset, managed a thin smile before turning and leaving without another word. The simplicity and generosity of this wonderful gesture left me speechless. As he climbed the gangway off the float, he turned and, silently, gave me a little salute. Looking down at the religious medal in my hand, I felt a lump in my throat. That morning, if I hadn't really believed in its power, I would have gone straight back up that gangway and headed for home.

This was no time to surrender to homesickness. Truly the wrong moment. I had to keep focused so as not to overlook a thing.

Taking out my Argos emergency radio beacon, I glanced at the instructions and activated the device. As soon as it started beeping, I knew it was perfectly ready to send a distress signal to rescue services. I stowed the last few provisions, hanging a bunch of bananas on a forward bulkhead so they would ripen slowly. Without saying a word, Georges — one of the people who'd opened their home to me on my arrival in Saint-Pierre — watched me work. Leaning on the railing of the gangway to the float, he looked tired. Fortunately for me, he'd always been ready to lend a hand. Leaving these new friends I'd made through the local Rotary Club wasn't going to be easy. Everything aboard *Pilot* was shipshape. Night had already fallen and I was leaving my "traveling companion" one last time before returning to her for keeps.

"You'll only spend one more night alone, *Pilot*. Starting tomorrow, we'll be like two peas in a pod."

Those were the very first words I had ever spoken to my boat.

At Olga's house, I ate my last home-cooked supper, and then slept in a warm, dry bed for the last time. She had graciously helped me in my preparations. Lord knows how many times during the crossing I would think back to that peaceful night! That last night ashore, I was trying to hide the fact that I was totally exhausted. Jean-Christophe, my photographer friend, had come over to spend the evening with me. I paced back and forth from one room to the other, putting my things together, nibbling a piece of cheese without even realizing what I was doing — I simply couldn't sit still. I wrote one last letter to my family while millions of things kept running through my mind. To boot, I had a stomachache. I kept wondering if the weather was right, if I was making the right decision. The French Meteorological Bureau had just called to tell me that the weather had deteriorated since the morning. That night I hardly slept. Under my covers, I lay coiled tensely, picturing the angry sea racing. I hoped I wouldn't suffer too much. I thought about what the island's policemen, sea rescue experts, had told me: stories of shipwrecks, of trawlers that had gone down because of the subzero cold. In a matter of hours, a layer of ice coats such a vessel; tons of ice form on decks, bulwarks, on the bow, rendering her so logy that she cannot move. In some cases, help arrives minutes too late, and then the rescuers can only watch as the ice-clad trawler sinks like a stone.

I thought back to the first fifteen years of my life, spent aboard a sailing vessel in the West Indies. Needing reassurance, I told myself that the horrendous events in the policemen's stories never happened in June. I searched for happier memories but still couldn't sleep. Fortunately, the story of my "survival suit" came to mind: my policemen friends refused to let me sail without one — in case I wound up waiting for rescue in 34 degree F (2 degree C) water. But I was reluctant to take one along because those so-called dry suits are huge and I had very little space onboard. Besides, I wasn't really sure I'd have enough time to don the suit before the boat went down. In addition, by the time any rescue vessel reached me, I would have died of hypothermia, suit or no suit. But seeing how much it meant to them, I finally agreed to accept it. The French immediately called their Canadian police counterparts, who came over from the mainland just to bring me one of the suits. The Canadians invited me aboard their boat for a "fitting." Comically bashful and awkward, they couldn't bring themselves to touch me. Maybe Canadian policemen weren't in the habit of dressing women. The man adjusting my hood was actually afraid to push back my hair to free it from the zipper. During the voyage, the survival suit was stowed within easy reach aboard my boat, and I could never see it without thinking of those men. But, that last night at Olga's, I was praying I would never have to use it.

After a near-sleepless night, I got out of bed. Breakfast was a hasty affair that we ate in almost complete silence. I couldn't manage to get a thing down. Then, abruptly, Jean-Louis and I left for the harbor.

That Friday, June 13, throngs of people crowded the floats of the Saint-Pierre Sailing Club. It was 8 A.M., local time — and really cold. Everybody was bundled up in thick down jackets. The wind was blowing at twenty-five knots — in the right direction — and that would help me get away from the Newfoundland coast. Ten-year-old Marie, whose class I had visited the day before, held out a rose for me. I fastened her flower to the little jackstay beside the banner of Saint-Pierre and Miquelon and the French tricolor, which was the flag Gérard d'Aboville had brought home from his Pacific crossing and had given to me.

I kept looking seaward: the wind had become gustier. I got into my safety harness and clipped myself to *Pilot*. This time, we were bound together, for better or for worse. When I slid my oars out, they seemed to weigh a ton. Jean-Louis Hardy, a friend from the Rotary Club, cast off the lines. At last, I was under way! Everybody clapped, cars honked; I heard the braying of foghorns mingling with the whistles from boats. I smiled so that the people watching wouldn't see my anxiety, but I could only wonder about the weather awaiting me and if I had made the right decision. I had to force back a sob, as jumbled emotions got the best of me.

Lots of fishing boats and yachts stayed with me as far as the Bertrand buoy. From there on, only the large French police vessel, the *Fulmar,* followed me out into the open sea. Along with my policemen friends aboard that ship was journalist Christian Bex of the media chain France Info (comparable to CNN), who had been with me for a week. In addition, Philip Plisson, Jean-Christophe (who never put down his camera), and the local police chief were there. They were escorting me — the big ship watching over the little one. But *Pilot* was being tossed around by the seas, so I had to pay close attention to my rowing. Quite soon, I wished that all of them would go back. I hated teary good-byes; the sooner we cut the umbilical cord the better. I started gesturing, clearly waving farewell. No, I wasn't going to cry with them watching me. And I certainly didn't want to get them depressed. Finally, they seemed to understand my wishes and turned around. The *Fulmar* gradually dropped into the distance. I started pulling toward the southeast, toward my goal. I was alone, truly alone.

*   *   *

I will long remember that Friday, June 13, 2003, my first day at sea. I won't ever forget that sudden loneliness or, after rowing nonstop for hours and hours, the way my palms bled on the oars. I won't forget how the Newfoundland coast stubbornly refused to disappear or how *Pilot* and I might have been dashed against its rocky cliffs at any moment. With each passing second, the situation became more desperate. I was near exhaustion but had to stay alert. There could be no rest until I gained enough sea room. That whole day, scalding tears ran down my cheeks, which were already coated with salt.

2

Sponsors and High Heels — The Fishermen of St. John's — Live from the Atlantic

I T W A S 7 A . M . and my fourth day at sea. The storm had finally moved away and I was rowing again. I had been in my little cockpit for an hour. I was sitting on the sliding seat, a thick foam rubber cushion under my rear. My feet were braced against the "stretcher," a transverse rod adjusted precisely for the length of my legs. In this way, rowing almost became a reflex, a conditioned response. I eventually got it down to a routine. At times, I even closed my eyes. My thoughts would stray and I literally forgot what I was doing. But those first thirty-six hours — before getting into the rhythm — had been harder than anything I'd expected, and by morning, merely gripping the oars became sheer torture. My palms were blistered, with salt getting into the raw flesh and creating deeper wounds. With each stroke of the oars, I tried to remember the precious advice I'd been given before my departure:

"Maud, don't squeeze the handles of your oars. Try to

imagine you're allowing the air to get through. Keep yourself firmly on the sliding seat by leaning outward with your oars."

I relaxed my grip on the handles as much as possible to prevent blistering, but I was gritting my teeth. I told myself that even this day would finally end.

For all of that, I'd had ample experience with blistered palms from rowing too much. Aside from all the dinghies and other skiffs I used to row — including that old tub my two brothers and I had when we lived in the West Indies — my official debut in ocean rowing came in 1999. That was the year I formed an association to get troubled youths off the streets and involve them in sailing or rowing a Bantry *yole*, a classic forty-foot open boat. On a year-round basis, we would take off for all points in France — and even abroad — to compete in races. This dear old longboat, pulled by ten oars, was wonderful training. Indeed, it was she that stirred my passion for ocean rowing. What I relish most about this sport is being so close to the water. I find this proximity enchanting, and it was the sensation I hoped to experience on this transatlantic crossing. During my training runs on the river aboard little *Pilot,* everything went beautifully. Weather conditions weren't a factor, as the river's surface was smooth, the sun was shining, and *Pilot* seemed to glide ahead by herself. I even managed to get her up to three knots on some stretches of the river. Later, during intensive training in Brittany, at Riec-sur-Belon, staying at the home of my friend Jean-Daniel, a bass fisherman, I was in peak form. I slept well and ate well. A chase boat usually came out with me, so there was no stress to be managed. If something went wrong, I simply waved my hand and somebody came along to help me. And I knew that at the end of each day I could warm up with a hot shower and sleep in a nice cozy bed.

But here, on the Grand Banks, with choppy seas, everything was different. The short, steep waves weren't allowing me enough time to use proper rowing technique. Far from making my work easier, the waves off Newfoundland were just plain unfair to ocean rowers. They couldn't care less if I knocked myself out stroking in midair because the blades of my oars clean missed the water. A lot the waves cared if I toppled off my sliding seat completely. What did it mean to them that my oars kept jumping out of my hands and banging me in the chest? They went right on doing their own thing. If that wasn't enough, the nastier waves would sneak up on us crosswise, smacking into the side of *Pilot* and tossing her around like a plaything.

Every muscle in my body grew tense, strained. Doing my best to hang on, the boat lurched, pitched, and shuddered. Her motion became frenzied, totally chaotic. Before my departure, Dr. Jean-Yves Chauve, the doctor who made sure I was physically fit, predicted that to provide the energy it took to hold my position I would need to consume more than one thousand calories daily. Now I really understood what he meant: merely keeping my place on the sliding seat became exhausting. The seat was soaked with spray, so I kept slipping off. My oars either buried themselves in waves that were too high, or the blades cut uselessly through the air searching for the ocean that had just dropped out from under them. It felt as though I were making zero progress. The hands of the chronometer on the instrument panel indicated I'd been rowing in those six- to nine-foot seas for three hours. Curiously, time — which had flown by while the boat was being readied for sea — now seemed to have slowed to a crawl. Luckily for me, I still had day and night, all other reference points having vanished. I tried not to keep my eyes glued to the chronometer's minute and second hands that barely moved. I forced myself to think about something else. Scenes from my departure paraded endlessly through my mind; when I saw all those faces I felt sad again. Breaking the bonds with the landed world hadn't been easy. And to think, I was just at the start of my North Atlantic crossing and this would go on for at least three months! But I refused to allow myself to cry.

I remembered being told that the first ten days were going to be unbearable. It would take that long to get your body under control, forget your old living habits, forget the comforts of dry land. I would need ten days to get used to the boat's incessant motion — and to adapt to the awful solitude.

I wanted to drop my oars. I wanted to slump down onto the floorboards of the cockpit and just sit there huddled up, out of the wind. I needed to be reassured, comforted, encouraged.

"Come on, girl, back to work. Get those oars moving."

I was talking out loud to myself, my tired voice sounding strange to my ears. It came from deep within me and had none of its usual cheerfulness. I had been nauseated since the moment I'd sailed. I had to get back in the groove.

Although weak in the knees, I managed to grab a can of a liquid nutritional supplement. Vanilla-flavored, it was supposed to be good — what was more, it contained everything the body needed. But I couldn't get it all down; the stuff hit my stomach with a thud. In a few minutes, the queasiness returned. On deck, it was bitter cold, an icy wind stinging my cheeks, so I drew my head down into my polar fleece scarf. Finding a bit of warmth there, I closed my eyes and tried to forget. But *Pilot* was yawing right and left drunkenly. This was no time to weaken. I had to get with the program. If I gave up now, I might not pull myself together.

Painfully, I began rowing again. At least it kept me warm.

The coastline had dropped below the horizon only minutes before. I had the feeling that an eternity had gone by since my departure. My chances of actually completing the transatlantic crossing began to seem more and more remote. Even making it halfway across appeared unlikely. I glanced at the chart — Europe was incredibly far away. I kept kicking myself for going on such a mad adventure.

There was only one source of motivation capable of forcing me to stick it out: I had to hang in there another week — until June 24. That was the date for broadcasting a ship-to-shore phone conversation scheduled by my cosponsor Buro+, an office supplies store. They were holding their annual meeting on that date and had invited Gérard d'Aboville to emcee the program with me "live" from the North Atlantic. Carole Gradit and Monsieur Ortola, the Buro+ manager, had thought of everything: models of the boat, posters, charts of my route to be given away as gifts to their customers. In other words, this was hardly the time to quit.

I remembered how those folks at Buro+ had taken the plunge with me — certainly, due in large measure to the Pilot Corporation, the pen manufacturing company and my first sponsor. But mainly, the Buro+ management believed in my plan. And for that I could never forget them. As for my relationship with Pilot, that all happened by chance, through a friend — I'd go so far as to call him a savior — Jean-Paul Degeorges. He spoke about my adventure to Marcel Ringfard, the company's manager for Europe. He, in turn, passed the file over to Hugues Chatelain, head of Pilot's office in France. I met him for the first time only a few days before the press conference, announcing my impending voyage. At the time I had no sponsor at all and was financing the whole project out of my own savings. The day of our meeting, I knew I had to be as professional as possible. It was essential to convince him there wasn't the slightest doubt about my chances for success, about my determination to persevere. In addition, I had to show him that the project was a sound investment. It took all my passion, enthusiasm, and determination to convince him. He fell in love with my audacious plan and agreed to commit his corporation to the adventure. No sooner had he given the green light than I rushed out to give the boat a new look. She then bore the name *Miss* and was painted red and black, my favorite colors. At 4 A.M., in the street outside the Maison de la Radio, hours before the press conference organized by my faithful partner France Info, we christened her *Pilot,* with a few passersby watching. The next day the boat was loaded aboard a container ship bound for Saint-Pierre and Miquelon.

At the beginning, when I was wandering around in search of sponsors, without contacts, I never managed to get past the switchboard operator or the assistant to the manager for communications. It was like running into a brick wall. But I made up my mind to continue at any cost. Obviously, one sponsor would lead to another, setting off a chain reaction: positive things were bound to happen.

I couldn't bear thinking of the mess Buro+ would be in if I gave up — after all the trouble I'd had talking them into this. I could hear it now: "Yes, uh, er, about Maud . . . well, actually, she didn't start off very well and she kind of overextended herself . . . so she's decided to come home." End of bulletin. I refused to consider this hideous scenario. They believed in me, and I'd be letting them down if I gave up only ten days into the voyage. I had to stick it out. I had to — at the very least, for Buro+.

It had been hard to be credible and convincing. I'd struggled against serious prejudices, against deep-rooted fears and doubts, against my own image as a young woman. Now was the time to prove to them they'd been right believing in me. As feminine as I was in tailored suit and heels, I could also face a challenge — namely, that of rowing across the North Atlantic. Willpower: I had it. But it hadn't been an easy matter to explain the sound reasoning behind my plan. I met with top brass — CEOs, business and marketing managers. Some seemed to agree to the meetings simply to humor me, as if they wanted to confirm their idea that the venture was out of the question. They'd certainly misread my letter . . . and misjudged me.

"Must be some kind of joke," they probably said. "No twenty-five-year-old girl could seriously entertain such an idea."

But I kept going to those meetings — at times blushing (to my everlasting shame) — but more determined than ever, armed with my file folder, my carefully reasoned arguments, my boundless enthusiasm . . . and the breakdown of funding needed.

As head of my own real estate agency, I was able to juggle my schedule somewhat (although I had to make up my time by working nights) which was a real break. In this way, I managed to move ahead with preparations for my big plan while still coping with my Paris properties. Between stints at the job, I would breathe deeply, don my sailor skin — better yet, my determination to make this dream come true. Then off I'd go to another appointment with potential sponsors. I had one mission and one mission only: to convince them, to show them that it *was* possible!

Over a thousand people have climbed Mount Everest. Twelve have walked on the moon. Only six have rowed the Atlantic from west to east. A woman has yet to accomplish this feat.

Their faces registered surprise as they read this first paragraph of my proposal aloud.

I let them go on and, then, as concisely as possible, told them of my passion, my determination, my burning desire to make it across the Atlantic. How many times I saw them smile, laughing at my audacity while looking me up and down. Some of them tried to picture me in my little boat when I showed them a photo of it. The only time my appearance backfired was at the weekly magazine *Madame Figaro*. Claudine Salmon of France Info, my first and most faithful media partner, had recommended me to the magazine. I think that Marie-Claire Pauwels, the editor in chief of *Madame Figaro,* must have been astonished; at the same time, she may have been flattered and pleased at being able to link the name of her magazine with the exploit of a young woman both athletic and feminine. First and foremost, she had decided to help a woman fulfill herself through a personal exploit. For once, the fact that I hadn't walked in wearing my red oilskin jacket brought me luck. But it seldom went that way, and in most cases, though I managed to keep a smile on my face, my blood was boiling all the same. Sad, discouraged, I heard them say to me: "We'll have to take a closer look at this. We'll be in touch with you. You must understand this is not the right time to take on any new projects; we've had several budget cutbacks this year . . . and, in any event, the budget has already been decided." They would manage to cut all our talks short without ever uttering the word *no.* I always went away with my face flushed and a stomachache.

My failure to come up with financing became really problematic; I had to buy the cheapest possible equipment, pare all my expenses to the bone. And, bottom line, it meant that I would go on working at the office right up to the eve of my departure. There was still so much to do. . . .

Indeed, the night of the *Madame Figaro* rejection, I had a meeting with the shareholders of a co-op building. I wouldn't be home before eleven. Here we were in mid-January, and every night when I got home I still had to send out dozens of proposal letters online. I was putting in really long days. My clients came into the real estate office and trooped into the meeting room. I had to avoid thinking about the transatlantic crossing if I meant to concentrate on my work as a building management agent. If those people had only known what I was planning! Though I doubt seriously they could have conceived of such a thing. I circulated the attendance list but, on one corner of my yellow legal pad, I was jotting something down: a reminder to drop a line to my naval architect about the question of small port-lights in the bulkhead. It was one of Gérard d'Aboville's ideas. He'd had them installed on his boat. A little hatch to let in some air without having to open the large one in very bad weather — seems obvious, doesn't it?

"Miss Fontenoy, just exactly why haven't those repairs to the stairwell been finished? For a week now we've been putting up with stairs that are half missing."

I was startled. I had to banish all thought of the boat, fast. I took a deep breath and put on my best co-op management agent face. Shaking off fatigue, I began explaining the stairwell issue.

We were getting through the morning; the sea had flattened since the day before, and the coast had disappeared. I was surrounded by nothing but ocean. The immense bowl of the sky seemed to be reminding me of my own small size. I still didn't dare look at the chart: I had pored over it too long before setting out and didn't feel like getting excited about it so soon. The sun rose, and I finally warmed up a bit. I pulled off my knitted cap and, bundled in two fleece pullovers and my watch coat, climbed into my little cockpit for a new day of rowing. This little space, which I also call my rowing station, was narrow and almost empty. Nothing but the oars and the sliding seat, something I had to get used to (on the Bantry *yoles,* the thwarts are fixed, not sliding). Mounted permanently in the cockpit was a compass given to me by the nautical instrument maker, Plastimo. This remarkable compass indicated my reverse course, a particularly useful feature since — like most rowers — I normally sat facing astern. And then there was my sophisticated Loch-Speedo meteorological sensor that gave me — well, was supposed to give me — the ocean depth, the water temperature, and my speed.

Each morning, I took my oars out of the forward cabin and then, each night, stowed them there again. They were vital. The French Rowing Federation had presented me with three pairs of them — just in case! In addition to space for the oars, the forward cabin held three lockers. The first one was devoted to provisions: freeze-dried meals, stowed in no special menu arrangement. Access to the locker was difficult: wriggling on my belly, I never quite managed to get anything out of there without bruising some part of my anatomy. I took only the number of bags needed for the week, digging them out at random. It was my little brother Roch (twenty-three years old, six foot two) who had made up the contents of the bags for me. Well, at least I had a surprise every day. The second locker held my clothing — mainly fleece pullovers provided by Marine Pool. They were vacuum-packed in plastic bags. Again, it was Roch who helped me pack them. Some of the pullovers were even perfumed, almost certainly my mother's idea. Every time I opened one of these transparent bags, I was greeted by delightful scents of land — not to mention the pleasure of finding something dry to wear. At sea, once you're used to the odor of iodine, everything becomes monotonous. It was as though I had lost my sense of smell. I dreamed of fragrant trees, freshly mown grass, and lilacs. The last locker, all the way forward, held my spare desalinator and its repair equipment.

Everything in the lockers was sealed in red and white watertight containers, thus constituting reserve floatation. This was one more idea from my father, a naval architect in his younger days. He gave me lots of valuable suggestions, but this particular one wasn't terribly practical. Each time I struggled to extract or replace one of these containers, I did think about him (maybe he'd meant it to happen that way), but I also swore like a trooper whenever I jammed a finger or barked my shins. Then I seemed to hear a tiny voice saying, "Quit grousing, Maud!"

The after part of the boat was my cabin: a cube measuring three feet on all sides. My whole world was squeezed into that tiny cubicle: my bunk with a mattress that was far too thin (it had already taken the shape of my body and made me feel as if I were sleeping on the ground); the galley (a stainless steel stove and teakettle); the electrical panel; my medical kit; the second Argos emergency radio beacon, my distress flares, and other safety equipment. From inside the cabin I could steer with my feet, just as I could from my rowing station (the cockpit).

My radar detector started to beep, indicating the presence of another radar set — that is, an approaching vessel. I scanned the horizon, turning my head in every direction until I finally caught sight of a white boat coming my way. I just went right on rowing. In fifteen minutes, it was nearly alongside me — a large trawler with two big arms, something like a giant spider. My mother's name appeared painted on her bow: *Chantal Spirit*. (It must have been Chantal's way of sending her regards.) Fortunately, the sea wasn't running too high, so I was able to look up at the trawler's crew. Five men in heavy yellow oilskin suits were leaning over the bulwarks, shouting down to me in English. They were Canadians out of St. John's, Newfoundland.

"What's happened to you? Do you need help?"

I saw their eyes, round with wonder. I could tell these Newfies were getting all set to tow me back to shore.

"No, I'm just rowing. I'm rowing across the Atlantic."

Although I'd spoken to them in English, it might just as well have been Chinese. Even I had trouble believing what I had said — that I was just starting out, that I wasn't far from my starting point and that, all things being equal, I would reach the other side in three months. They still looked worried, so I went on: "No problem. Don't worry."

They still didn't seem to understand, repeating four or five times: "Do you need help?"

I started rowing again to show them that everything was all right and that they needn't worry. They had been ashore that very morning and would be back on land that night. I'd been out five days already and they insisted on seeing me home.

"No, really, everything's fine."

I realized that they couldn't figure out how everything could possibly be stowed in such a small space. Actually, I had enough provisions for ninety days aboard my boat. Still, I was kind of scared: first of all, they were men and I was a female — alone. The minute I'd spotted them coming closer, I had pulled on a thick sweater and my watch cap to conceal my hair. I had also put on sunglasses, trying to camouflage my face as much as possible. I didn't want them lowering a boat to see me up close. I was being cautious, having no wish to tempt fate. In addition, I was afraid these Newfie fishermen might very well use force to bring me back ashore. I knew how easily my situation could be misunderstood: they probably thought I was completely insane.

I wanted out of there; I couldn't stand being confronted by civilization again. I was sick of hearing these Newfie trawlermen urging me to give up. Now they were even pulling out cameras — doubtless scared of not being believed when they got back to St. John's. The trawler was so close that her nets, suspended from those huge arms, were directly above me. I was shaking a bit and, to make it clear that our chat was over, I gave them a friendly wave. When I began rowing as hard as I could, they all wished me a good trip. They followed me for a while, watching me pull away but keeping their distance. Then they stopped and began setting out their nets. Gradually the trawler grew smaller and smaller and I was plunged back into my solitude.

In the days that followed, the temperature dropped, shrouding me in dense fog. When June 24 came — the day so long anticipated — I was exhausted, constantly drenched, and frozen. Although I'd been out at sea for only eleven days, it seemed like an eternity. I had my long-distance call from Buro+ at 10 P.M. At the appointed time, I plugged in my Iridium satellite telephone, turning it on at the very last minute because I had to go easy on the batteries. The sun had appeared too infrequently for the solar panel to recharge them. At 10:01, I was waiting for the phone to ring, my lids growing heavy as I struggled against sleep. Minutes went by, a quarter of an hour, a half hour. My phone still didn't ring. The idea that they had forgotten me made my blood run cold. I'd held out these last few days for their sake! They couldn't pull a stunt like this on me now! All of a sudden I felt terribly alone. The cold had an edge to it; the night was totally dark; and the silence eerie. Only the tiny flashing white light atop the jack-stay kept me company. At 11 P.M., when I was on the verge of despair, they called. Having gathered all their customers in a large Deauville restaurant, they had just finished their meal and, in the cozy warmth of the room, hadn't quite gotten around to calling me. Please! The contrast was almost surreal. Shivering with cold, I snuggled against my sodden eiderdown quilt, drinking in their words like delicious nectar. Teasing me, Gérard d'Aboville began by reading me the dinner menu. I think it was the chocolate éclair that made my mouth water most after eleven days on my diet of freeze-dried powdered food. But, I have to admit, Gérard did make me laugh; he made me relax, and that was his intention. For fifteen minutes, I completely escaped from my boat. I was with them, surrounded by their warmth, picturing them in minute detail, and most of all hoping for only one thing: that they wouldn't leave me right away. But I knew we would have to hang up soon. Answering their questions, I sensed that they, too, were moved at hearing me "live" from the North Atlantic, surrounded by icebergs. Our call reached its end. They sensed that I couldn't bear putting the phone down. Roger Ortola got on the line: "We'll be seeing you when you get in, Maud. Don't worry." He was trying to cheer me up, boost my morale. But no one seemed to realize the distance I would still need to cover. I had to smile at their enthusiasm. They believed in me and that was very good to hear. I tried to keep up a brave front, quipping, "Thanks for calling. Do think of me while you're licking your plates clean."

With those words, I glanced at my larder of fresh fruit, which had already grown moldy in its hammock nets.

3

Fog on the Grand Banks — Childhood Memories — Near Miss — First Bath — Jellyfish for Company

*T*HE WIND WAS STILL BLOWING HARD that morning. I had been under way for nearly three weeks. The cold was so bitter I had yet to bathe a single time — and what's more, I hadn't washed my hair. It was quite a while since I had had a bath, but I was afraid of getting sick.

At the rate I was moving over the Grand Banks off Newfoundland's coast, the crossing would take far longer than expected. Theoretically, the detour south around the icebergs shouldn't have taken me much more than ten days. But those ten days became thirty and that meant suffering in the cold. And all kinds of problems began piling up. Ocean temperature went down to 38 degrees F (6 degrees C), and during the night the thermometer had registered 34 degrees F (2 degrees C) inside my cabin. Outside, the wind blew so hard it shook *Pilot* from morning to night, which often kept me from sleeping.

To top it off, the fog was so dense, I could barely make

out the forward end of my own boat. The two of us were trapped in this white hell. With each stroke of the oars, we groped ahead, plunging a little deeper into the dismal stuff.

At times I was so scared of moving deeper into the fog that my oar strokes became timid. I felt as if I were drowning. The air was almost too heavy to breathe, suffocating despite the cold, as if the whole weight of the sky was on my chest. When, in a matter of seconds, the fog would re-form and close behind us, I felt as though I were penetrating the deepest part of a forest where trees, like the jaws of an animal, snapped shut on me, stifling me.

Without a ray of light filtering through, it became darker and darker. I began wondering if I would ever see the sun again. All I had was my compass to guide me. I could not bear any more of the fog. Not being able to see more than a few yards ahead of you can cruelly affect the mind. I missed seeing the horizon. I was being crushed between these white walls, between these barriers of dense fog. The wind kept on rising, chilling everything in its path. I began to think it would turn *Pilot* and me into one solid block of ice. If only the wind could carry off that fog!

"What do you think, *Pilot?*"

Pilot gave no answer.

I became increasingly silent. My throat was so parched that merely opening my mouth was torture. I'd been rationing fresh water ever since the departure. Speaking was what one did in the normal world, but it was just the opposite out here. I felt as though I were on another planet — no sound emerged from me. This reality had me in its clutches and I wanted out. I sat there, huddled up, trying to forget. Things couldn't go on this way — it had to stop. I was shivering and my stomach ached. Feeling completely lost, I sought refuge from the icy wind in my thick scarf. My throat tightened, tears came. I was hiding. But what was I hiding from? The sea? How would it look if the god of the sea knew I was scared silly? Neptune only liked sailors with guts. He liked brave mariners, the ones who fought back. He couldn't stand losers, fatalists. I began rowing harder. If, just then, somebody had asked me to speak, I would have snapped, given up completely. I tried to concentrate on my goal, of the happiness awaiting me on the day I would come within just a few miles of the European coast. Yes, I could see the finish. I could imagine hugging my family. But I could not shake the feeling that I'd been at sea for many months instead of three weeks.

The wind was still blowing hard, entering everywhere, creeping inside my jacket, nipping at my hands, my nose, my cheeks. I felt weak and dizzy. I was throwing up everything I ate. Every morning, it was the same thing: although quite empty, my stomach turned itself inside out like a glove. I wondered if it was the vitamins that I couldn't tolerate. I decided to stop taking them to see what would happen.

Now and then a wave — larger than the others — completely submerged the cockpit. Then I was soaked from head to foot. But I always made sure to bundle up before going out on deck, for, as I said, I was deathly afraid of getting sick.

I felt so very alone. Once a day, for a few minutes, I

phoned land. It would be even worse afterward, but at least for those few minutes I felt that I was with my family, close to them. When I hung up, a mighty shove sent me tumbling back into my solitude. This time, Mother didn't have her usual voice, so I knew I had to try to reassure her, tell her that I was coping.

"Yes, yes. I've been eating."

"Are you drinking? You have to force yourself . . ."

That one I dodged. Because there hadn't been enough sunlight to recharge the batteries to run the desalinator, I'd cut back drastically on the amount of drinking water I consumed. Instead, I dictated my logbook to her so that she could put it on my Web site. Funny, how I couldn't bring myself to use the pronoun "I." It was almost as if *I* had been detached from who I was. I told my story in the third person. To be as objective as possible, I made myself into an external observer, viewed from above, separate from the suffering of the body that I could see struggling alone on that wide sea. Writing as if I were telling someone else's story was clearly a way for me to protect myself, helping me to put my "misfortunes" into perspective.

For months, this would be the rule: a complete gap between me and the people on land, snug in their warm houses, unable to imagine the conditions in which I lived. They worried day after day, feeling guilty at not having managed to keep me locked up at home. As a matter of fact, I was infinitely grateful to them for not standing in my way — they understood my motivation. In all likelihood, any other attitude on their part wouldn't have changed my mind. Honestly, that's true. When you're ready to row across an ocean, you're supposed to be able to handle looks of disapproval. Otherwise it's a sign you're not ready and will probably crack in mid-ocean. My parents set the example for me. They had a dream — that of raising my brothers and me in a special way — and they lived their dream to the fullest, never fearing what others might say.

While I was actually born inland, smack in the middle of the French countryside, I was born a second time. This "re-birth" took place six days later when my parents carried me aboard our sailboat, the fifty-one-foot schooner my father had built two years earlier. I lived aboard my family's boat for the next fifteen years. We sailed the waters of the West Indies, stopping wherever we liked — at times staying for months. I never went to a real school before the twelfth grade. We took correspondence courses under my father's vigilant eye. We studied *every* morning. For us, there were no weekends or va-cations. In the afternoon, we played and swam. We went for walks on the islands, gathering mangoes and guavas along the way. We were highly self-reliant children. In a manner of speaking, we were brought up the hard way, but a concern for freedom was always with us. I remember that whenever my family boarded other sailboats for a visit and we children got tired, Father would simply tell us, "All right, lie down over there." And in two seconds, we were curled up in a corner with the voices and laughter of the grown-ups lulling us to sleep. What great times those were! Now, as I rowed *Pilot* — hungry, cold, tired — I told myself that my special childhood had been the best possible training. I wasn't out here on the

North Atlantic as some kind of lady rowing champion. I'd been trained to be a "tough cookie." As a little girl, whenever I fell down and hurt myself, my father would tell me: "Stop crying." And then he'd get me to think about something else.

After my mother got my logbook entry for the day, we always talked a bit. Clearly, she was worried, even if she attempted to hide her fears from me. I tried to cheer her up. While crossing the North Atlantic, my family couldn't share my daily trials. At any rate, burdening them with all the details wouldn't have changed anything. Instead, I asked about their comings and goings. Had my brother Roch passed his exams? Had they begun making over that room for the baby Yann's wife was expecting? Chantal told me that she was picking out the colors and had bought a nice wooden crib. I did want so badly to be with them when the baby came. Hanging up at the end of a phone call was the hardest part, but I played the game all the way. When I stowed my phone, the real trouble started. I clung desperately to the memory of their every word, as though by remembering, I could keep my family with me a little longer. To hear their voices as if we were in the same room one minute and then to be so far from them the next — this made it even harder. I should have limited the number of calls, or not called at all. But, living in a world of instant communication, everybody wanted to know what was going on aboard *Pilot*. If one day went by without a logbook entry posted on my Web site, it was a calamity; pandemonium ensued; family and friends began sending e-mails expressing their concern. Slipping right back into my solitude after these conversations became impossible. It would remain a problem until the end of the voyage.

*　　*　　*

It was the middle of the night. Noises came from the cock-pit; someone had gotten aboard *Pilot*. Clad in green and black camouflage fatigues, a machete sheathed on his hip, a fierce guerrilla from the jungle was trying to force his way into my cabin. Unable to get the hatch open, his fist pounded on the Plexiglas bubble over me. I woke with a start, my heart pound-ing. Was someone there? No, it was just a nightmare. But something was indeed happening: the sea was crashing over the boat, burying her under green water. It was another terrible night. I thought my spine would break from *Pilot*'s plunging and kicking — clearly, my mattress was too thin. Topside, a driving rain was getting into the cabin. With the condensation, everything inside was sodden. Soon day would break, but I still couldn't see much with the damn fog that never cleared. I huddled in my eiderdown, my ears and feet frozen. My tiny cubicle was dank, airless, and musty, the cloth-ing and pillow moldy from the dampness. Night on *Pilot* was a horror. All day long I lived in dread of the coming of night. I tried not to think about it. But as it drew inexorably nearer, finally the point came where I couldn't stay on deck any longer. I was forced to retreat to my wretched shelter, cold and damp as a grave.

Night in fog was so frighteningly dark it has to be expe-rienced to be believed. Ashore, no darkness is so intense, so terrifying as that which you find at sea in a fog. Without the slightest glimmer of light, imprisoned in a world completely beyond understanding, we drifted toward our fate. I was ter-ribly worried about colliding with icebergs, a number of which had been reported around me. But I hadn't sighted any as yet.

Pilot wouldn't stop her rolling and lurching; I wedged myself into my bunk with foam rubber, but that didn't do any good. Hanging on that way, every muscle in my body was strained with the boat's violent motion. And lashing myself to my bunk was out of the question, since untying myself and escaping from the cabin in an emergency would be far too complicated. I kept being flung from one side of the cabin to the other. I just wanted to sleep.

Measured against the total time estimated for this transatlantic crossing, sleep was a bonus — it represented a few hours of oblivion. Yet within that, every fifteen minutes or so, I was jolted awake by a wave larger than the others, by a quickening of *Pilot*'s motion, by drops of water pelting my face. The din in the cabin was excruciating. Slabs of water rushed at us, rumbling like runaway trains. It was as if I were inside a drum, so loud was the thunder of the breaking seas against the hull. The rollers crashed down on us tirelessly, the wooden hull groaned like a living thing, the steering gear kept banging. I scrunched even closer to the bulkhead, my head aching. I was barely able to breathe. I just wanted to bring back a piece of silence, to hear nothing for a few minutes; I couldn't bear any more of this noise that left me trembling with fear. I wanted night to end and day to break.

Dawn made its appearance. I was waiting for it, watching for it as it crept in, a timid glow in the thick fog trying hard not to be seen. But then I pounced. It was six o'clock — time to start work. Actually, that didn't mean I wanted to start work. As wet and cold as my aft cabin was, it was still better than being in the cockpit, always so full of water and exposed to the wind. But I had to keep making progress and get out of this fog-shrouded area. I'd already been on the Grand Banks for three long weeks, pulling hard for the south, trying to skirt the icebergs, and my route eastward to France hadn't even begun. I tried to forget that the whole blasted crossing still remained to be done. Why the devil had I made the decision to sail from Saint-Pierre and Miquelon? That is, so far west of Cape Race, which is on the tip of Newfoundland and is the easternmost point in North America? Most sailors start at Cape Race. By leaving from Saint-Pierre I had rowed an extra three hundred miles. At times, I had trouble remembering why. In any case, it was an original choice of starting place, and, for that at least, my solo crossing would be unique. This notion made me smile because, obviously, all voyages were unique. On the ocean, no two trips could ever be the same.

Little by little, I eased myself out of my cabin. I made a face as I brushed my teeth — I was using seawater.

This morning, the sea was jet-black; it looked heavier, thicker than usual. I had the feeling Neptune wanted to make things even harder for me than he already had. He didn't seem to want to let me get by. Aching and bruised all over, I had blistered palms and my backside was rubbed raw. The blow I'd gotten during the last storm had left my face misshapen. One cheek remained so swollen that the sight of it revolted me. Fortunately, my wrist felt better.

But my hair, matted with the salt and moisture, had become really intolerable. I was so filthy I no longer felt human. Me, who would never go out without wearing perfume! I had been so feminine! Now I could hardly remember myself from that remote time. I was learning to forget "the old Maud," learning to forget my body, my femininity. I was concentrating on my goal, on retaining the motivation that I had honed so carefully before setting out on my journey.

I will never forget that October day, about a year earlier, when the voyage was decided. It was the day I made a down payment on the boat, the day I realized I could never back out. I spent the rest of the day shut up in my house alone, listening over and over to the same Tracy Chapman record. I plumbed the depths of my soul, pondering the transatlantic crossing at great length, weighing my motives, my strength, my potential. I had to be certain; I had to be really honest with myself. Weighing the pros and the cons, I considered what I stood to gain — and what I stood to lose. I put myself through a real third degree. That day I really made up my mind. *I knew.* I knew that I wouldn't change my mind.

The voyage had been a dream at first, the dream of experiencing something great on the ocean. Ever since my family's return from the West Indies (to take up residence aboard a canal boat in France), I kept going back to the sea. First, there was sailing, and then, ocean rowing. But I wanted more. I had this unsatisfied desire to experience a great adventure. And I meant to experience it all alone, to drive myself to the limits, put my emotions, my body and its potential, to the test. And then to keep on going. I had dreamed about the exploits of the explorers; I'd followed the adventures of Gérard d'Aboville, but had also read the stories of great sailors such as Bernard Moitessier, Joshua Slocum, Alain Gerbault. I had read the novels of Melville and Jack London — even Joseph Kessel's *Les Cavaliers,* which, although set in the mountains, is the story of a struggle with the human body and the demands put upon it. Now it would be my turn to set out on an adventure of my own. I knew only one factor would allow me to see the crossing through without giving up: my willpower. Only from this would I find the strength to go on.

Now, on this white-fog morning on the Grand Banks I was still trying to reason with myself: I was focused, my body was strong, and it would heal. I used my body like a precious tool, taking care of it so that it wouldn't become a burden. My body wasn't the boss; it didn't make the decisions. Its moaning and whining weren't going to make me lose my nerve.

I was in the midst of these thoughts when my radar detector went off: a ship was in the vicinity. Since we were right at the border between the Grand Banks and the open sea, it might not be a trawler this time. I couldn't see a thing through the thick wall of fog. The beeping became louder. I looked around sharply, but didn't know what to do. The ship was getting closer, though I couldn't tell where it was coming from. After a few minutes, the beeping grew continuous. The ship had to be very close, but over the roar of the breakers I couldn't hear it . . . unless the wind was carrying the sound of the ship's engines away. Yes, I could already smell its exhaust fumes. I held my breath, straining my ears. My heart began beating intensely. Suddenly, I could hear the ship — I heard its engines throbbing off my port side. When the noise came closer, my limbs began to shake uncontrollably. Was the ship coming right at me? What was I supposed to do? Jump in the water? Scream? The idea of shooting off flares occurred to me, but I quickly ruled it out. Flares were a distress signal; they could be taken as a call for help. No, impossible. As a rule, the man on the ship's bridge should have seen me on his radar screen. (I would learn subsequently that my own radar set was defective and detected no vessels during the entire crossing.) But maybe my tiny craft was just low in the water, too close to the surface. On their radar set, *Pilot* and I appeared as just another wave. From the throb of its motors, the vessel had to be large — maybe a freighter or a container ship. I dove into the cabin and grabbed my pilot charts, the ones showing the main shipping lanes.

I was back on my sliding seat, studying the charts. There shouldn't have been any vessel where I was, but this ship was probably circling the Grand Banks, trying to avoid icebergs. To me, sitting in the cockpit, time seemed interminable as I went on straining to hear if the throbbing was getting louder or fading away. The noise of the ship remained steady — coming at me. Too weak in the knees to stand up, I sat there, every muscle taut, tense. Then, in a panic, I started to "dog down" all my hatches. If the ship overturned me, at least I could still climb back aboard — that is, if my boat wasn't smashed to bits. Most important, I couldn't allow *Pilot* to be capsized with her hatches open. I could phone my loved ones ashore, but that wouldn't change a thing. Anyway, I'd made a promise to myself not to tell them about dangers or hardships I encountered. I went on waiting, watching *Pilot,* and listening. There it was! From the noise of their engines, they had to be astern of me. There could be no mistake about it. I could tell they were gradually pulling away from me, and I started to breathe again. I glanced at my watch: the near miss with the ship had lasted all of fifteen minutes, but those minutes had seemed like an eternity, and now I felt completely drained. A rude awakening, but at least it was over.

That business had given me an appetite. I had a small quantity of non–freeze-dried food aboard and I pulled out one of those bags. In it, I found a package of prunes. They were supposed to give energy, right? As I ate them, I thought over what had just happened. What if I had been in the ship's path? Given the number of vessels plying the Grand Banks — I'd heard talk of about three hundred Canadian boats, plus Spanish and Portuguese ones — I would really need to watch my step. I might not be so lucky next time. From this point on, I began keeping vigilant watch. The thought of a swim in that icy water — even before breakfast — could take away one's enthusiasm for rowing, couldn't it?

Around noon, I'd had it. Even if it meant coming down with double pneumonia, I had to wash myself. I had no way of knowing how much longer I could tolerate the fog. But I did know one thing: if I intended to keep my sanity, I had to start looking human again. I had reached the point where I just couldn't tolerate it anymore; I was suffocating under all these layers of filth. All right, granted there was a chance I might get sick, but there was also the risk of having to give up because I felt so uncomfortable in my own skin.

Pilot went on rolling and pitching — would it ever stop? They were reporting high winds for the following day and I had no way of knowing if the rough weather would last several hours or several days. So if I meant to wash myself, I had to do it right away; afterward, I might be forced to stay penned up in my cage for as much as forty-eight hours. And that would be out of the question, given my foul, unwashed state. At any cost, I needed to feel better in order to get through my next joust with the North Atlantic. Case closed. I got my things ready.

I quickly pulled a vacuum-packed bag containing a dry towel out of a locker, then a tube of shampoo and cream for very dry skin. When everything was set, I knew I had to go for it. As I began stripping off one fleece pullover after another, I realized just how cold it was. Standing up in the cockpit, I reminded myself of that basic law of the sea: one hand for the ship, and one hand for yourself. I therefore made sure to hold on to my little jackstay as *Pilot* lurched and rolled. Shivering, I was gooseflesh from head to toe. As a fine rain began falling, I stood there, stark naked, in a twenty-five-knot wind, ankle-deep in the water that invariably sloshed around in my rowing station. Let's just imagine, it's a wintry day and you're waiting at the bus stop or on the train platform early in the morning. With your eyes still full of sleep, you're bundled up in your coat, slapping your sides with your arms and rubbing your hands to warm up. What if you were asked to parade around nude in that kind of weather? As for me, I took a couple of deep breaths and forced myself to sing and shout. I tried to think about something else, psyching myself up as best I could. The fact was, I had to go through with this bathing idea if I hoped to avoid serious skin problems — namely, boils. I drew one bucketful of icy seawater and gingerly began to wet myself. Definitely not my idea of fun. I yelled at the top of my lungs in an effort to forget the excruciating cold. The water felt like fire. My body had still not adapted to such harsh conditions. My mind flashed back to that last hot shower I'd taken before the departure. Why hadn't I really savored it? I didn't realize how lucky I was at the time.

After a while, the cold simply anesthetized me; I felt numb. I rushed, rinsing myself at top speed. Then, as fast as possible, I grabbed my towel and rubbed myself frantically from head to toe. Next, I applied a generous layer of the dry-skin cream. In the blink of an eye I was fully dressed again, back in my warm Marine Pool 100 percent polyester clothes and my perfectly designed polar fleece pullovers. But I was shivering uncontrollably, my teeth chattering to beat the band. After drying my hair as much as possible, I slid into the cabin for a nap, exhausted.

Heavy raindrops pelting the deck jolted me awake about an hour later. Leaks began to appear everywhere. I scrunched against the aft bulkhead trying to protect my dry clothes. It was dismal watching the rain running over the glass bubble above me, but I did feel better — it was about time. I was glad I'd had the courage to bathe. I just wanted to warm up a bit before returning to my oars — that is, if it ever stopped raining. I would also have to dry out my towel because I only had four of them to last me through the entire crossing. I daydreamed for a moment — about a ray of sunshine.

Lying on my back, my head deep in a dry fleece pullover, I began to warm up. With both feet up, jammed against the overhead to improve circulation in my legs and to ease my aching muscles, I ran my eyes over the cabin. To my left was the electrical panel to which the solar panels were connected; the light on the Active Echo radar transponder was flashing green — that meant no vessels in the vicinity. To my right, the liquid-filled compass swung to the rhythm of the waves. Next to it, the handle of the diving knife in its sheath made a dark spot. There was also the little stove and kettle, a waterproof flashlight and my big spoon for stirring freeze-dried dishes. That was my whole galley. In the fruit nettings I'd suspended, only a single lime was unspoiled.

This transatlantic voyage was going to take forever. It was only 9 A.M. and it felt as if I had already put in an entire day. I grew absorbed in contemplating the drawings that were pinned up around the cabin. They had been made by children at the schools I visited prior to my trip. Using paints and crayons, they had made me pictures of flowers, trees, and smiles; and some, in a childish hand, had written "Good Luck," and "I love you." One girl in the class had created a particularly compelling montage. Using photos cut from fashion magazines to form letters, she'd spelled out Maud. Without realizing it, I extended my forefinger, to trace their outlines. I could see their smiling faces, their mischievous looks. My visits to those school classrooms had been an extraordinary experience.

The first visit had been to a secondary school in Paris, the Collège Jules Romain, where I lectured on desalinization by the reverse osmosis system. I'd never taught in a classroom before. The kids couldn't believe their eyes. I put up a chart of the Atlantic and astounded them by unveiling my machine for desalinating seawater. I also showed them several freeze-dried

dishes to give them a better understanding of my provisions
for the crossing. Then, in each of the classes, I sparked a de-
bate lasting roughly an hour about all aspects of my plan. I was
really impressed by the students' thinking, by all the questions
they managed to come up with. I remember one boy's perti-
nent question as to whether I planned to take along bottles of
oxygen in the event I was forced to stay penned up in my
cabin. It was great fun sharing my adventure with them. It
was an opportunity to show them their wildest dreams could
come true — if they were extremely careful and prepared
everything thoroughly. And, deep down, each of them had a
dream. For some, it was of becoming a professional soccer
player; for others, it meant becoming an archaeologist, veteri-
narian, or, perhaps, owning a horse or a giant panda. My adventure had made them dream; they imagined themselves
stroking dolphins and watching whales. After all, what could
be more exciting? Seeing their enthusiasm lent me the wings
to show them my goal, to breathe courage into them, enabling
them to attain their own goals. Everything was possible. They
simply had to believe — really believe — in their aspirations
and learn how to obtain the means to achieve them. After
all, it's up to us to put some gusto in our lives. But, that said,
be forewarned! Certain watchwords — caution, careful pre-
paration, attention to detail, hard work, courage, and willpower — go hand in hand in realizing a dream. The students
gave me their rapt attention as I explained that, to realize my
dream, I had to start by drawing up a plan. It hadn't been a
matter of leaping into space with my eyes shut. I told them
that at the beginning, I had been up against a mountain. So

first I cut that mountain into pieces, then divided it into stages. And then, slowly, I worked on each of those pieces, one by one — giving it my all. Most important, I told them, they couldn't become discouraged and, on that score, it didn't matter how long it took.

My gender raised another question for the students. I'd come to the school straight from my real-estate agency. They saw me dressed like a businesswoman — in all probability, just like their own mothers. And yet, there I was — talking to them about capsizing, violent storms, emergency repairs. . . . Baffled, they asked me if I had any children. They seemed to be saying that a woman like me wasn't really a woman, a woman who could have babies. Mothers couldn't be adventurers who wanted to row across an ocean! And in one sense, they were right. I wouldn't have run that risk if I'd had a row of curly-haired cherubs like them at home. I'd met some other blond youngsters in Saint-Pierre and Miquelon while visiting a kindergarten class. One was more adorable than the other. Their eyes were wide with wonder. For them — and it was clear at that time — I was an extraterrestrial. I showed them the ocean, but they couldn't comprehend the distance involved. To explain how long three, maybe four, thousand miles were, I said that crossing the Atlantic would take me as long as all their school vacations rolled into one. That seemed to make an impression. But they seemed most interested in fish, dolphins, whales — and in knowing whether my mother would cry if I never returned. Touchingly enough, their questions were connected with feelings, unlike grown-ups who asked mainly about technical matters.

So that the Web site tracking my transatlantic crossing

might interest them, I made up a wild love story involving Josephine, a flirtatious jellyfish — and a romantic rowboat. Each day in the logbook that appeared on the Web site, the children followed the adventures of Josephine, a trifle on the lazy side, and the rowboat who took care of her. It even got to the point where young Internet surfers would sometimes write to my webmaster, Alain Rigal, astonished at learning I wasn't "alone" onboard. It was a fact that, while in the fog, loneliness, and monotony of Newfoundland's Grand Banks, the only living creatures I saw were dozens and dozens of jellyfish of all sizes just below the water's surface.

It made me feel blue now, thinking back to those wonderful times with the children. Like a little cheering section of my own, they had all turned out on the pier, shouting: *"Bon voyage, Maud!"* Seeing them there had given me such a lump in my throat. Now, I had these memories to keep me company over the coming months. The memories were my horizon in that eternal fog, my rays of sunshine, my bits of warmth in the cold. And, someday, I would have children of my own. . . .

Gradually, on July 14, Bastille Day, the fog began to lift. I had just left what they called the "tail" of the Grand Banks and was now in a deeper area of the ocean — more than twelve thousand feet deep. Overnight, I entered the Gulf Stream, a warm current that would give me a welcome eastward push. After rowing for a whole month, I was only just now beginning to head for the land where the morning sun came up.

"Course due east, full speed ahead!"

Part Two

Misleading Sun on the Gulf Stream

4

Letter from d'Aboville — Life aboard *Pilot* — A Shipyard in a Field

*I*T WAS AS IF MY EYES WERE OPENING for the first time. A beautiful day was emerging. Some magic wand had made the pea-soup fog around me disappear. The surroundings I cherished — the sea so near to me on my little boat, the sea that could never be closer — all of that had returned.

With a smile I remembered how my dad used to tell me that, as a baby, my toes had developed in much the same way as fingers for most people. Learning to walk aboard a boat, I took my first steps on rolling, pitching decks, so I instinctively looked for toeholds. I was almost certainly built for life on the water. Obviously, there was great risk attached to what I was doing — but what a delight to be on the sea. I saw the sun shining on the boat, giving the day a joyous touch. Almost at once, I felt my spirit invaded by the warmth. Sunlight, at last! My solar panels would now start functioning, my battery would begin recharging and, with a little luck, I might actually dry out my things. It would also help chase the dankness from my cabin.

Now I would be able to drink my fill of water, although my body had grown used to water rationing — I was somehow less thirsty than before. I seemed to need fewer things to keep going.

Once my eyes had adapted to the bright daylight, the color of the water astonished me. The ocean no longer resembled the lard-colored magma I'd been rowing through since my departure. It was now a deep, shining navy blue. Its surface scintillated and a long groundswell replaced those short, choppy waves I'd had to put up with on the shallower areas of the banks.

But what astounded me most was the temperature. The air had finally donned more summery garb (it was, after all, late July) and the water temperature had all at once climbed to almost 80 degrees F. Stunned by the incredible speed of this change, I immediately powered up my global positioning system and plotted my position on a large chart of the Atlantic. No doubt about it: I had found that well-known current, the Gulf Stream. Exactly as I'd learned before setting out, this warm water mass didn't mix with the cold water owing to differences in density. Setting to the east, the Gulf Stream would carry me home to France faster and was decidedly something I meant to hang on to. By indicating the water temperature, my Loch-Speedo helped me shape a course to follow these warmer waters.

A pleasant thought crossed my mind just then and, without delay, I plunged my hand into one of the lockers. From a large waterproof envelope, I pulled the letter Gérard d'Aboville had written to me before I'd set out. On the envelope, he'd made the notation "*Not to be opened before your arrival in the Gulf Stream.*" Tearing it open, I hurriedly read the lines written by my godfather or, as he liked to say, my technical advisor: "*Well done! Now it's the open sea . . . it's dolphins, flying fish, and other creatures. . . . But don't dawdle, it's getting later into the year.*" His words really touched me. For a moment, I was back on land with the people I loved. But I also felt a twinge of sorrow. I had just completed the first lap of a hard race — I'd made it to the open sea. But this had taken me a full four weeks. One might say my trip to France hadn't yet begun. It felt as though I were starting out a second time. After thirty grueling days at sea, I looked at my chart, then at the horizon, then back at the chart again. I couldn't believe what I was seeing: still five thousand kilometers — three thousand miles — to go! For a minute, the stats discouraged me. But I tried thinking about reaching my next big hurdle — the halfway mark.

I was in a new world, dazzled by the lavishness of nature, by the spectacle of glorious skies each morning. What a shock to see after my colorless world of the first four weeks. I began to observe the complex displays offered to me. I nourished my spirit with all these details, these combinations of colors and variations in the weather.

For the first time, I felt accepted, as if I had passed my exams, and now the wonders of this world could be revealed to me. The ocean became a person, a friend with whom I shared my thoughts and feelings in the logbook. It was all-powerful. Its charisma and strength made me tremble, but its secrets fascinated me. I had fallen in love with the ocean; its beauty left me stunned. True, the ocean had made me suffer, had caused me to cry with pain and fear. It had tried to discourage me, and it had forced me to lose my temper, to concentrate, to struggle against giving up every minute for the last twenty-nine days. It had obliged me to expand my limits. I had been hurt, so badly, it was unlikely I would ever forget it.

But today the ocean seemed ready to make amends, to reward me for my efforts. It was revealing its good side. And what a good side! Each morning it amazed me. The first orange gleams of the sun would pull me out of my sleep. Opening my eyes, I watched the orange gradually transform, turning a hue more vivid and bright. Greedily, I drank in those colors, those vitamins. I yearned for them, and their memory would remain imprinted deep within me. This helped me endure the days, so harsh and full of pain. All the stories the ocean told me were exciting, one more than the other. Most of the time I daydreamed, as my arms did all the rowing, moving back and forth mechanically, and those dreams allowed me to play hooky and run away with the ocean. At night, the radar detector permitting, I made sure that these wonderful escapes didn't end, and I would slip away from the boat for a visit ashore. The day before I embarked, I'd gone by my house to take a shower. And I'd visited Gipsy, my brother's girlfriend, to see how she was coming along with her pregnancy. I never stopped thinking about Yann and her. She was expecting in early September. I'd be back in time for that blessed event, for sure.

That morning, while seated at my rowing station, I was jolted by the sound of two powerful explosions. I looked around, stunned. There was nothing on the horizon. The sky was serene, perfectly empty, a uniform turquoise blue. Flabbergasted, I phoned my friends on shore to tell them about the strange detonations, but nobody could explain the cause. Chantal got the idea of putting this question on the Web site. And, a few days later, I got the answer. It was the Concorde, the very last flight of the Concorde. It had broken the sound barrier in that lonely sky, directly above me. A member of its flight crew, back on the ground, had found the question on my Web site.

In the afternoon, I rowed silently, grimacing because of the terrible pain in my back and my rear end. It was time for a break, but my hour — yes, I took a rest every hour — wasn't quite up. I kept going for those last ten minutes and, I must admit, each minute was sheer torture for me. But I had to hang in — every stroke of the oars brought the coast of Europe closer. I reminded myself that what I did today wouldn't need to be done tomorrow. Finally, at 4:01 P.M., I let my oars droop against the sides of the boat and stood up to rub my sore buttocks. Holding on to the boat so I wouldn't fall overboard, I looked up.

This was one of the lessons I learned on the water: look up, look at all those things we forget to see on land, with this life of ours that slips faster and faster through our fingers, this life that carries us along without giving us time to catch our breath. I gazed up into the immense expanse of the sky. Large cumulonimbus clouds were on the horizon, forming a white jewel-box setting for the turquoise sky. With their long horizontal base, they seemed to have been generated all at one time. The more I studied the clouds, the more they seemed like fresh whipped cream — they made my mouth water. The sky was disturbingly serene; I wouldn't have believed that such a sight could exist. Wherever the sky had none of those whipped-cream clouds, it seemed covered with the icing a baker might put on a cake. I thought back to my grandfather, a baker, and how on Sundays he would make marvelous pastries for our family dinners. I remembered how he used to call me his "doll." Who would have dreamed that the little girl in the lovely dresses would end up alone in a rowboat in mid-ocean?

The sea, still rough, also seemed to find the clouds appetizing, reaching up and licking them every now and then. In hardening myself to take responsibility for my own decisions, to stay the course, to keep from cracking, I'd had to learn to forget my body. For a second, I was almost afraid I had done so at the cost of my sensitivity. But just then I was experiencing more delightful sensations than those most people ever experience in normal everyday life. Learning to withstand suffering had transported me to another plane. Not that I had attained truth, but I had experienced the beauty that surrounds us. On land, I had never imagined I would cry at the sight of the setting sun. Yet, after so much heavy weather, this is precisely what happened to me that evening, amid the immensity of sea and sky. I found a great tenderness within me, yearning for expression. For the first time in years, I was coming out of my shell, my emotions close to the surface. That evening was magical; something truly incredible had taken place before my eyes. My gaze fixed on the horizon, I finished the day's rowing. Though it was sundown, today I would get no show; the sky was covered by a thick grayish cloak. *Pilot* heaved slowly in the long swells as night fell. This is what happened. In just ten minutes a band of light formed between horizon and the woolly mass of the clouds. The sky parted just at the height of an immense and majestic sun. It resembled an eye, opening suddenly, its pupil a fascinating orange-yellow. I was enraptured, mesmerized by this fiery eye. For a matter of seconds, its flame-red outline illuminated the horizon in an arc of more than 180 degrees. An intense emotion went through me, one I would have loved to share with someone else. The sea engulfed this eye that seemed on the verge of tears. Then the sky closed up again, leaving me bewitched by the eye's mysterious appearance. After such a spectacle, one understands just how small we are. As I watched the sunsets of the passing days, I never ceased to marvel at their beauty, and this helped me cope with my daily existence.

Let's talk about that daily existence. I was beginning to adapt to my boat. I knew *Pilot*'s every feature by heart. I had become used to the harsh, comfortless life in my aft cabin. I had gotten my bearings, found landmarks, organized myself. Endeavoring to forget the noise and not to get angry about *Pilot*'s incessant motion, I went with her movements instead of fighting them. I tried not to let the impossibility of bathing irritate me. I didn't allow myself to think of a good salad or a glass of orange juice. I couldn't afford to think about these things if I meant to complete the voyage. My life was geared to the weather. There were times when I was penned up in the cabin for twenty-four to thirty-six hours — and sometimes forty-eight hours — at a stretch. I had to wait for the rough weather to pass through so I could leave my cramped space. At times like that, times of forced solitude and immobility, panic is no stranger. You have to find something, anything, to think about, to imagine. I could describe the least little irregularities in the overhead of my cabin. I knew the ingredients of all my freeze-dried dishes by heart. I studied everything from ten different angles. For example, the logo of my media partner, France Info, held no secrets for me, which made the company's top exec, Michel Polacco, laugh when I told him. I imagined the story behind that logo; I never tired of staring at the way the O was designed. I thought about the designers who had created it, about whether or not they'd submitted several drafts. Anyone else might think this completely insane . . . and I wasn't far from thinking the same thing.

On the phone with my mother, I was greedy for details. On land, nobody understood my questioning, but in mid-ocean the need to know every detail about what they were doing, what they wore to the theater, what tasty dishes they'd eaten — microscopic details I'd never considered before, made sense. I needed to fill my mind with picture postcards about their lives.

Four months of solitude — it's endless. So I thought about the future, too. I made plans. Even as I was being thrown every which way by rough seas, colliding with bulkheads in the cabin, I daydreamed constantly. At times, the aft cabin became the equivalent of being inside a washing machine. In these situations, losing your patience or getting upset isn't an option. You could never tell how long the rough weather might continue. Would it last another hour, two hours — or three days? The question was all too vague. So I tried to relax.

I really dreaded container ships. The chances of them seeing me, especially in storms, were small indeed. The risk of a collision was inherent in this type of crossing: I traveled at all times in the main shipping lanes. Over the course of the voyage, I was to pass more than fifty ships. Every time my radar detector went off, I'd stick my head up inside the Plexiglas bubble to see the vessel triggering the alarm. I could see them passing me in the distance. But at times they were uncomfortably close.

One morning, after a night in twelve-foot seas, a large cargo ship (longer than a football field and a half) brushed past us. For reasons unknown, it didn't have its radar set on and, accordingly, no signal warned me of its approach. I often think back on that scene. Only the throbbing of its enormous engines made me stick my head up, and then I saw it — a huge iron monster painted red. Good God! My blood suddenly rushed to my head. I stood there, mouth agape, unable to make a sound. This all happened in the space of a few seconds, given the ship's terrifying speed. No sooner had I seen the ship than it was past me. I collapsed in my bunk. We'd almost been rammed. In the Mid-Atlantic, such an accident would prove fatal. It took me the whole day to get over the scare. Why hadn't those seamen turned on their radar? But if you thought about it seriously, radar or not, the situation would have been the same. The sea was too rough to take my place in the cockpit and, even if I'd run that risk, the wind and waves would have made it impossible for me to control the boat. It was terrible, the boat was drifting, at the mercy of the elements; all I could do was start praying not to be run down by freighters.

When not penned up in my wet cubicle, I had to make up for the time lost. As soon as I was awake, I started brushing my teeth, washing my face; I got to work without delay. Generally speaking, I started rowing at 6 A.M. This was especially true in the Gulf Stream, where some absolutely cloudless days were just too hot. At such times, it bordered on lunacy to stay out in the midday sun. I felt roasted. I wore long-sleeved shirts, a peaked cap, sunglasses, and a thick coat of sunscreen. But that didn't stop me from having terrible migraine headaches every night. I came close to sunstroke and sometimes had to take shelter between noon and 2 P.M. My cabin was about 100 degrees F (40 degrees C), two or three times hotter than the cockpit. But as the cabin was the lesser of two evils, I stayed in there. Naturally, taking a swim was out of the question (I sometimes saw the fins of sharks).

My basic diet consisted of powdered, freeze-dried food. At the beginning, I had different kinds of soup, cereal bars, dried fruit, and one chocolate bar per week. But very soon I realized that this was too little nourishment. I was consuming enormous amounts of calories just to keep my head above water; meanwhile, I rowed eight to ten hours a day, which was quite a lot. I needed sugar, energy — and pleasure. Which was something I had underestimated. My freeze-dried dishes were packets of powdered food that I rehydrated with the water created by my desalinator. I won't say that it was bad — actually, I even thought it was good. With the passage of time, it got better. The farther I got from land, the more I appreciated some of my food items. My brother Roch had bought fiber bars, which I had considered inedible (and, for that matter, so did he). I stowed all of them away, in the bottom of a locker. After two months, however, when I had nothing left but strained food, they tasted just fine. I even managed to devour an entire fiber bar between two strokes of my oars. I would never have believed that I could enjoy them so much. As a rule, though, I ate only at mealtimes, trying to keep on schedule. Looking forward to meals gave me something to think about, but I also had to ration my provisions. I got plenty to eat, but since my boat was small and only finite quantities of provisions could be stowed, I did need to watch what I ate.

Pilot has an overall length of twenty-four feet (7.50 meters), and her beam is four and a half feet (1.60 meters). That isn't big. Empty, she displaces about 770 pounds (350 kilograms) and, fully loaded, 1,320 pounds (six hundred kilograms). I can assure you this is heavy, a lot of weight to push. For this reason, I made a careful analysis of what I should — and *could* — take along. This was especially important, because I didn't intend to throw anything over the side during my voyage. Those of us who really love the sea can never bear to jettison an empty plastic bottle or a single ounce of garbage. As I crossed the Atlantic, I carefully placed those items in a special container in the forward compartment. Naturally, access to other lockers became more and more difficult as the time needed for my crossing stretched out.

In the cabin, the first-aid kit alone took up an entire

locker. That left me only four spaces in which to stow the tool chest, food for the week, clothing, safety gear, navigational equipment, and, naturally, all the instruction manuals. I took these along to make sure I could repair anything that broke down. As you will see, they would prove extremely useful in the middle of my voyage. *Pilot* was built inland at a yard in Boran-sur-Oise, right in the middle of a farmer's field, thirty miles north of Paris. She was built from the plans for a boat that had crossed the Atlantic by the southern, or trade-wind, route. On the basis of these plans, I worked out several design improvements with Gérard d'Aboville; most of all, we wanted to make her stronger, as she would be facing the storms up north. We began by increasing water-ballast-tank capacity. When filled with seawater, these tanks below the waterline serve to make the boat heavier in storms and help right her in the event of a capsize. We also tried to reengineer the cabin design so that life onboard might be less dismal (though there's only so much that can be done). Often, my father, Marc, joined me at the yard to monitor the construction process. I stopped by very early almost every morning, just before going to work at the real-estate agency. I had wished I could drop everything and do nothing but supervise the building of the boat for four months. I wanted to see everything, know everything about her — almost like watching a child grow. Unfortunately, I still didn't have any sponsors and I needed my job to pay for the boat.

Pilot's preliminary trials were carried out near the locks of a canal in the countryside. Local residents who watched the event found it hard to believe that this tiny craft could brave the immensity of the ocean. "That's madness," they kept saying. We carried out righting tests: I got in the cabin and then we rolled her over using ropes. I recall that everybody got a laugh out of that. I knew there were people watching and this changed my perception of things. These righting trials went quickly, however, and I didn't feel all that much anxiety either before or after. True, *Pilot* took on some water through the air vent, but we had ample time to work out the glitch. There weren't any other problems.

With regard to the comfort factor, on the other hand, nothing had really changed. My list of do's and don'ts for surviving aboard *Pilot* at sea are: 1) Be satisfied with very little; 2) Don't drive yourself crazy thinking about your life before the crossing; 3) Whatever you do, don't get the urge to go for a walk. I really did miss walking, not being able to get up and stretch when I was confined in the cabin. However, before starting to row each day, I forced myself to do sit-ups. This was to avoid getting too many charley horses or pulling a muscle. And I did the same sit-ups at night: discipline! discipline!

After every hour of rowing, I massaged my legs to get the blood circulating, and I also forced myself to drink. The water from my desalinator was undrinkable. Unlike the food that I wound up actually enjoying, the desalinated and de-mineralized water proved vile. My guess is that when the water-making system was being installed, some epoxy resin must have dripped into the jerry can, polluting it. That chemical taste was what I couldn't stand. Although I forced myself to drink the water, I twice experienced cramps in my thighs that woke me with horrific pain.

"You've got to drink more, Maud," the doctor told me again and again, on the phone.

Such was my life aboard *Pilot*. I watched time drag by and tried to make do with little pleasures I found in witnessing the captivating purity and diversity of nature. I tried not to forget that, with every passing day, my dream was coming true.

I went on rowing tirelessly, staring into the distance.

5

On the Whale Highway —
Tropical Storm Dany — Dolphins

*A*N UNEXPECTED SOUND yanked me out of my sleep. It was like some kind of deep breathing. I scrambled out of my eiderdown and rushed topside half-dressed. There, I saw two shiny black masses — whales — bearing down on me, side by side. They were displacing vast amounts of water: their heads created huge bow waves and, behind, they left wakes of an amazing width. Measuring twice the length of my boat, the two leviathans kept right on coming with alarming serenity. Having never seen a whale up close before, I clung to the jackstay in my rowing station, rubbery-legged, trembling, my heart pounding. Since the ocean seemed to belong to the whales, I felt a little embarrassed to be in their path. Absolutely nothing could have stopped these gleaming, sinewy bulldozers, these immense locomotives from hurtling down the rails. I was torn between wanting to let them come even closer and wanting to frighten them off. Powerful geysers of water sprouted out of their thoracic cages. This was, I realized, the strange sound that had awakened me. The twin black masses effortlessly plowed ahead, to within thirty yards of *Pilot*'s hull. Witnessing such a sight, a delicious shiver ran through me. This was why I was out there, why I'd struggled with my doubts, against my fear of the unknown.

Had they seen me? And were they going to sound at the very last minute? Marine biologists claim whales are perfectly aware of their imposing dimensions and are skilled divers. Yes, but what if they didn't see me until the last minute? What if they miscalculated the distance and just happened to brush against *Pilot?* At their speed, we would be splintered, turned into match sticks, sent straight to the bottom. The immense flukes of the first whale smacked the surface of the sea, creating waves and sending a shudder through *Pilot*. Then, finally, I got a grip; I made a decision. I started clapping my hands and yelling. The scene must have been ludicrous. As if my pathetically feeble noisemaking was really going to stop those giant creatures! I imagined a spectator — way up high — witnessing this spectacle: me, alone, and half-naked on the blue immensity, a tiny marionette gesticulating at two black monsters approaching, unperturbed, at full speed. But from such a vantage point, that spectator might also see other whales, lots and lots of other whales. For all I knew, I might have been sitting above an entire pod, or family, of whales. Almost certainly, these two were attracted by *Pilot*'s fluorescent orange anti-fouling paint. All my efforts to catch their attention were for naught, however, and at this point, I seriously began to panic. My throat was sore from yelling; I didn't know what to do. Then, just before they broadsided me, both whales nosedived right under my keel. I actually felt the second one vibrating under my bare feet — and presto! — they reappeared on the other side of the boat, just ten or twelve yards away, as if nothing had happened. My legs gave way and

I landed on the cockpit sole. There was just something funny about their attitude. They almost seemed to be playing with me. Rather angry, and at the same time, amused, I shouted their way: "Hey, you think that's funny?"

That seemed to slow them down; I couldn't believe it. What was this — some kind of game? Or were they simply bored? In any case, they lolled, surrounding my tiny craft for a while, seemingly taken aback by my presence. I wondered what they were thinking. Certainly, they weren't at all afraid of me. For a few minutes, I felt less lonely, less gloomy. But I had to get going; the route was still very long. At 7:15 A.M. on that July 20, I climbed back into my seat and started my day's rowing. In silence, the whales turned around, going off on their mysterious way, leaving only the broad wake that would soon be the only trace of their passage.

Toward the end of the morning, I stopped rowing and switched on my cellular phone. It was time for a scheduled interview with Christian Bex, the journalist from France Info. I thoroughly enjoyed our weekly conferences and looked forward to them. And, of course, the chats got me away from my daily rowing sessions. Gérard d'Aboville had arranged an introduction to Christian, who'd covered his solo crossing of the Pacific Ocean in 1991. Thus, France Info became my partner and had stayed in my corner ever since. I gave Christian weekly reports from my watertight cabin, trying to be as calm but also enthusiastic as possible. I would tell him what I felt, trying to get him to share my dream for a few minutes, but he was becoming concerned that I wasn't confessing my fears or doubts. More than the media coverage, what really counted for me was hearing someone's enthusiasm. Christian's boss,

Michel Polacco, also phoned regularly to encourage me and give me news from the France Info staff. In those days of solitude and adversity, the calls were precious. My friends' words, simple as they were, cheered me enormously. They proved I hadn't been forgotten, that people still believed in me.

But, my satellite phone had scarcely flashed on when it started to beep. It meant that a fax message was coming in. It had to be a report from the meteorological bureau; I'd gone three days without hearing from them.

> Watch out, Maud. Tropical storm approaching. Dany is arriving in your area.
> Wave heights forecast 12–15 feet, wind fifty knots. Good luck. We're thinking about you.

I read the message over and over . . . tropical storm . . . good luck . . . Sure, that was easy to say. I had a hunch I was going to need that luck. Fifty-knot winds — the equivalent of one hundred kilometers per hour. I recalled that such weather conditions had forced Tori Murden, the Kentuckian, to give up her bid to cross the North Atlantic — and this, despite the fact that she'd gamely held out for eighty days. The news about tropical storm Dany spelled trouble. Somehow, this message and the two confirmations that followed were too timidly worded. I could tell that, behind their computer keyboards, my friends from Saint-Pierre didn't dare give me the bad news. I could imagine them drawing straws to decide who would have the painful task of writing me. The last message wasn't even signed. I would later learn that at this juncture everyone on shore was convinced I would give up that night. Saint-Pierre and the whole Newfoundland coast were on the alert, asking the weather specialists for news of me every hour. My photographer friend Jean-Christophe laid siege to the Meteorological Bureau of France. Back home, relatives and friends started biting their nails. Marc scanned one weather Web site after another to get more information, trying to find out just how long this storm would last. If only it were short-lived and could be as far as possible from me! It was late July and I'd been at sea for five weeks. I was scared of what might be coming.

From then on, things quickly began to deteriorate. The sky clouded up, darkening until it seemed to have changed to stone. At first, a veil was drawn across the sun; then it died like a candle deprived of air. A malevolent force had driven out the day and convulsed the ocean. *Pilot,* on the back of a sea monster that was just waking, shook harder and harder. Wearing my safety harness — the lifeline that kept me tied to the boat — it would soon be time to take shelter in the cabin. I watched anxiously as the sea turned the color of anthracite. My palms burning, I rowed for my life, desperately trying to drive the boat ahead. Naively, I believed I could still escape the punishment that awaited me. Yet I knew that the situation was evolving too fast — I couldn't possibly outrun the storm. The wind had already turned against us. It lashed the bow of my boat, preventing me from holding to my course. I had just pulled on my watch coat when the storm broke over me.

And then, magically, under a driving rain with the wind rising, a whale surfaced not sixty feet away. I nearly jumped out of my skin. I hadn't heard the sound of his blowhole while pulling at my oars. His wet black back almost as high as *Pilot,* he swam majestically alongside us. For a while, mesmerized by this apparition, I became oblivious to the storm. Long minutes went by before the whale sounded, returning gently to the depths.

"Awfully sorry," he seemed to say timidly. "Sorry you can't dive and take shelter at the bottom with me."

Wave heights forecast 12–15 feet, wind fifty knots. I decided to stow my oars in the forward cabin. In ten or twelve minutes, my whole world had turned black. This was no ordinary storm; the angry wind lashed us viciously, each wave seeming intent on splitting *Pilot* in two. I felt utterly alone and weak with fear as I shut myself up in the aft cabin again. In its dank gloom, I'd have to ride out this blow. I had no choice. I ached to have somebody at my side, somebody who could say a few words to reassure me. I tried to get away from myself for a while, tried to visualize a quieter, less frightening world. But then my lungs started begging for oxygen in that airless cabin. When the sea unleashes its fury this way, keeping your composure becomes a major problem. *Pilot,* tossed up on the crests of waves, then came crashing down in their troughs. I didn't know how to position myself to keep from getting my back broken. I wanted to scream my despair to the ocean, beg it to stop. My whole body had become an open wound. And those headaches nagging me!

Now at the mercy of wind and waves, I forced myself to think about something else, anything else. To forget the fury of the sea, my mind fled back to land; I made a beeline for those pleasures I missed so much: the cool tiles under my feet, the smell of an apple tart baking in the oven, the voices of the people I loved, jogging on a beaten earth path through a forest that was heavy with the fragrance of flowers and trees. I dreamed of having a few minutes' respite from the roar of those breaking seas, from that incessant motion. As the storm raged on, I clung to daydreams about the voyages I'd make and the children I'd have. My eyes half-closed, I clutched at the idea that I had a future waiting for me, that my life wasn't ending here and now.

Pilot lowered her bow and then, tremblingly, descended from the crest of one gray-green mountain to the valley below, so noisily that she seemed to be rolling down a gravel path. She kept on building up speed as if, by hurrying up to the top of that next oncoming hill, she could make that one the last. But the storm went on unabated. Inside the stuffy cabin, I hung on for dear life.

My radar detector started beeping. That was all I needed now — some hundred-thousand-ton container ship! I didn't even have time to dig out my flares. She was already on top of me, passing so close that, within seconds, I was gaping at an immense wall of iron rising starkly to starboard. I was so paralyzed with fear that I forgot to hold on and promptly bashed my head against the Plexiglas bubble when the ship's wake threw *Pilot* on her beam-ends. I thought I would burst a blood vessel. Why had that stupid ship been so close? And, on top of that, she passed at a good clip and just went on her way as if nothing had happened. The whole crew must have been below-decks where they could see nothing. So they'd never seen me. I failed to understand why my radar detector had warned me so late.

All that night, in terrifying darkness, I watched through the Plexiglas enclosure for the lights of ships, and was often flung against the bulkheads. Bruises and lumps covered my body — I had hideously scarred knees from using them to wedge myself in. I didn't dare doze off on the bunk. Eventually, the hours began to go by, but the storm lasted thirty-six miserable hours before the wind abated. Little by little, the seas began flattening out. But I remained in a state of shock. I felt traumatized for life; unable to collect my thoughts, I doubted I would ever get over it. I even lacked the strength to pick up my phone to reassure my family and friends ashore. Not a sound would come out of my mouth. Utterly paralyzed by fear, in the grip of my emotions, I remained huddled up in the cabin for a long time.

With a long swell still running, it was several hours before daybreak. Throwing off its deathly dark veil, the sky was once again shrouded in dense white fog. The sun stayed hidden all day, the ocean retaining the color of metal. I couldn't stop seeing images of cresting waves: walls of water fourteen to eighteen feet high barreling down on me (with hate or indifference? I wasn't sure). I kept on seeing the devilish beauty of the breaking waves as light traversed them for an instant, turning them turquoise, clear, perfect. I went on hearing the deafening thunder when they broke, converting the whole ocean into one misty, white, frothy surface. I had to get these scenes out of my mind.

Finally, I decided to phone my family to tell how I was

doing. But the tenderness of a human voice at the other end of the line brought a lump to my throat. My voice barely audible, I had to hang up quickly to avoid bursting into tears. Sharing my pain with loved ones only made matters worse, and I retreated to my bunk telling myself that things would get better the next day. I was utterly drained of energy and rest was imperative. The storm had been harrowing. It didn't matter whether or not I ever woke up: I just wanted to sleep as long as possible, to try to forget what had happened.

It was mid-afternoon when a new and different strange noise pulled me from my sleep. A high-pitched pinging sound, like an electronic gadget — maybe sonar — was coming from somewhere. Looking at my instrument panels, I couldn't identify this noise; it didn't seem to be coming from the boat. Then just where on earth was it coming from? I yanked the hatch open and popped my head out. The sea had calmed down and a ray of sunshine was peeking through the mass of clouds. And then I saw them: dolphins. Eight or nine gleaming dolphins rolled and plunged around *Pilot*. These big creatures — probably porpoises — were having fun swimming back and forth under the boat. Had they been attracted by the sound of my rudder slatting from side to side? Or was it our fluorescent orange hull? White flanks phosphorescent, snouts glinting in the sun, they had surfaced to play. When I put my hand into the water and shook it, they approached to touch me. It was almost electric. In an instant, my mind and body were filled with happiness. I felt tension ebbing from the muscles in my face. Amazingly childlike, the porpoises seemed to be smiling. They chuckled and made funny little cries, pleased that the storm had abated. I was fascinated by their fluid grace as they leaped and cavorted about. What amazed me was that with all their gamboling, they managed to avoid landing on top of each other. They paid close attention to their neighbors so as to keep out of the way. They nimbly crossed paths without touching, although sometimes their heads gently brushed. The previous day and a half of impossible weather abruptly vanished from memory. I couldn't have devised better therapy. I felt as if I were in a fairy tale, where there was always a happy ending. The only thing missing was Prince Charming.

Along with the warmth of the sun, the dolphins had brought me happiness, reassurance, and most wonderful of all, I was a trifle less alone. I was happy and, probably, a little proud of having faced my fears and doubts about getting this far across the ocean. What a nice present! The dolphins stayed around, playing for a little while, and then, one after the other, went leaping away. A splash or two for each and they were gone. I would encounter dozens of dolphins on my crossing. Often in the evening, while I watched the sun go down, they would draw near the boat. Sometimes, I could hear them in the distance as they went on their way. But I had never seen so many of them all at once, so close, so friendly.

My oars were waiting for me. I took a few deep breaths and did some warm-up exercises. My back and shoulders ached. All the same, I gazed lovingly at the water. I had already stopped being angry at the sea for what it had done to me. The sea has a way of winning you back.

Gwenbleiz, a fifty-one-foot stay-sail schooner built in the middle of farmland. I was carried aboard her when I was only seven days old and spent the next fifteen wonderful years on her in the West Indies.

My two brothers, Yann and Roch, and my mother in the cockpit. They're admiring the catch of the day: a large barracuda.

A dream existence: the hammock slung between our two masts. Yann and me cuddling with our father, a modern Robinson Crusoe.

Correspondence school in the morning; the beach, walks, and fruit gathering in the afternoon.

My second passion after boats: horses. Dressage or trail riding. Here I am in the mountains, by a campfire, beside the horse.

Growing up in a well-traveled family.

Action, my thirty-six-foot Bantry yole. Aboard her, inner-city youngsters had the opportunity to sail in races in France and abroad, which provided fabulous training in solidarity, cooperation, and teamwork. Ten rowers, a crew of thirteen, and our battle cry: "For a free State of Brie — Action!"

A few days before the departure, meditating at Pointe du Diamant on the island of Saint-Pierre. Jean-Christophe had come along to keep an eye on me. I felt a mixture of doubt and apprehension — even anguish — but my burning desire to be out on the ocean pulled me like a magnet.

All the gear aboard my tiny craft, *Pilot*, just before setting out: freeze-dried food, clothing, emergency equipment, Argos distress beacon, medical kit, quilts, sea anchors, gas bottles, stove.

Friday the 13th, at exactly 8 A.M., starting out from Saint-Pierre and Miquelon amid the applause of my new friends. I was both relieved to let the lines go and perturbed by the weather forecast, worse than expected. I was afraid of being driven back onto the rocky coast. My first capsize came two days later.

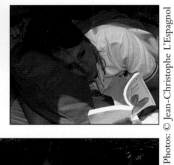

Life onboard in a space roughly three-by-three feet. I was forced to lock myself up inside this cabin for interminable days without a breath of fresh air.

Eight to ten hours of rowing daily on a boat weighing 1,500 pounds at the time of sailing.

Setting sun over the North Atlantic, vivid colors all around, a sight that will light up my dreams forever.

Photo taken during a late-August storm with thirty-foot waves and fifty-knot winds, seventeen capsizes, twenty-four hours of hell, on the brink of panic, my face swollen by salt and tears. I have never cried so much in my life.

My stock-in-trade for a month on Newfoundland's Grand Banks: a wild sea, fog, freezing temperatures from the presence of icebergs, container ships that I could hear but seldom saw.

Twenty-eight hundred miles alone under oars. The worst was never knowing if I would make it.

©Jacques Vapillon

October 9, 4 A.M., off La Coruña, Spain.
The finish was a powerful, unforgettable moment — a dream come true.

The following day, family, friends, and
Jean-François Copé were waiting for me at Orly.
Many of us burst into tears.

Gérard d'Aboville, my
godfather, technical advisor, and friend — the man
who crossed the Pacific,
rowing — was the first to
believe in this project
while others were saying
that it was no voyage for a
woman. I am indebted to
him for much, much more
than his advice; I will
always be grateful that he
never doubted me.

With my friends from
Radio France. Jean-Marie
Cavada who, six months
before, had opened the
doors of his Maison de la
Radio to me, and Michel
Polacco, CEO of France
Info, who followed my
progress over the ocean day
after day. I might have
succeeded without them —
but today you wouldn't
know anything about
my crossing.

Twenty-four feet long, with a beam of five feet,
three pairs of oars, and an ocean to cross.

*　　*　　*

All through late July and the whole month of August, I tried desperately to catch a fish. The idea of eating something fresh, something solid, made my mouth water when I got up each morning. I was fed up with my powdered, freeze-dried food. Jean-Daniel, my fisherman friend, had rigged several fishing lines for me. I set one up, a trolling line — not with bait, but an artificial lure. We'd see what would happen. I never took my eyes off the line as I rowed. If a fish struck at the lure, I couldn't afford to let it get away. I set out a line every day — not always the same one. But nothing happened, not so much as a bite, not an old shoe, not even seaweed, *nada, niente, nichts.* It was beyond frustrating. Back on land, they'd told me this would happen: you had to be going at least 6 knots to catch anything when trolling. With a maximum speed of 1.5 to 2 knots, some chance I had! It was a pity, though — I couldn't stop fantasizing about some lovely sushi or a big seafood platter. If that weren't enough, the people ashore didn't believe that I couldn't catch a fish.

To think that before setting out I bet my dad that if I managed to catch a fish, he would have to meet me at the finish line and bring me what I liked best — a bottle of fresh milk. And I mean *real milk.* Not just any kind, but the real McCoy straight from the cow, unhomogenized, unpasteurized — milk that was still warm.

That night, a flying fish landed in my cockpit, but it was so tiny that I threw it back in. It was a tough break — I sure wasn't going to get that bottle of milk. Well, when I got back, I'd just have to go get some myself at a dairy farm.

Another day, I pulled up alongside a turtle that was swimming just below the surface, his head above water. Maybe catching a turtle would make me eligible for the prize, I thought, so I brought it aboard for a closer look. The turtle was about a foot and a half in diameter, with a lovely brown-green shell. I kept it aboard for a few minutes and then, at the risk of losing that bet, put it back in the water. Somehow, the idea of making turtle soup didn't really appeal to me that morning. I was surprised that the turtle didn't pull its head right back into its shell. The turtle stayed nearby for a few minutes, his astonished little head turned toward the boat. I'd become attached to him. Incredible, what loneliness can do.

Before starting out on the crossing, I'd foreseen different problems, but not that one. I knew I was going solo but never imagined that loneliness could become a main cause of distress. We often picture solitude as something calm, tranquil; we see ourselves sitting in a field, with a good book in our hands. Silence, serenity, the singing of birds. But that isn't solitude. Solitude is hard, bitter, insidious. It's noisy, cruel, brutalizing. It's painful. When the ocean becomes stormy, when we feel insignificant, lost, when we are no longer in control of anything, that's solitude looking at fear, looking at death. I realized the degree to which I needed others, their presence, their faces, their smiles, gentle words, and even less than gentle ones — at times like these, gentleness wouldn't matter. We just need *someone*, it's as simple as that. We're social beings; now I know what this really means: we draw a kind of life force from others. I suffered from not being able to share anything — neither beautiful moments nor horrific sights. Facing problems alone, dealing with them when we're alone, always seems more complicated. We realize at those times how much the face of another helps us overcome our fears, our doubts. I had the feeling of an immense void within me, I felt drained of something. And yet, I'd always wanted to experience this adventure alone.

To cope with my solitude, I made up stories: I had only to close my eyes and I could see my younger brother Roch again, the way he sat on the Plexiglas cover during training sessions in Brittany; I saw the way he clapped his hands to time my strokes. But naturally it was only a daydream, a thought snatched from my daily existence, ephemeral and gone all too fast. I had to open my eyes, often full of tears, and keep on going. Grab those oars; don't get discouraged. The route that remained to be covered was long. My God, how long!

6

Longitude 31° West — A Bottle at Sea — End of August

*I*WAS GETTING CLOSER, stroke after stroke; yes, there was no doubt about it: the halfway mark was approaching. I was almost afraid to believe it. It was August 5 and, for a week already, communication had been telling me *You're there.* Yet, no matter how many times I plotted my position on the chart, it still wouldn't come out that way — I had yet to reach that coveted meridian of longitude: 31 degrees. Again, this was because of the capricious weather. For a week the wind had been up to its old tricks. I hadn't been moving east very fast to begin with, but now this wind kept shoving me back across the line. It was as though I was running a marathon, completely exhausted, and the finish line kept moving farther away. I swallowed my anger, redoubling my efforts to keep from giving up. I battled the waves, trying to keep my easterly heading. Most of all, I tried not to think about so much more easterly space to be covered, so many thousands more strokes of my oars, and Lord knew how many gales to be endured?

"Let's get past that imaginary line and then we'll see." That was what I kept telling myself. I thought of Sisyphus, the boulder he had to push up his immense mountain. Each of us has his mountain and each his burden. Now, *Pilot* became heavy pushing. I had the feeling that she weighed tons. All my efforts seemed useless. I felt like an ant caught in a honey jar.

To make matters worse, the wind began to freshen dangerously in the afternoon, kicking up waves nine to twelve feet in height, so it became impossible to stay topside. The waves broke over the cockpit and *Pilot* was completely awash. I daydreamed about being transported electronically to Noumea.* I shut myself up in the aft cabin; everything was soaked. It was dusk, the sky already dark with clouds. Waves smacked against our hull, making droplets of condensation fall on my hair. A shiver went through me, and I pulled my head down into my quilt. My feet were frozen. I rubbed them against each other in an effort to warm up. Again, I found myself scrunched up; again, I was flung from one side of the cabin to the other. No doubt about it: my bunk hadn't been engineered for the kind of weather I was getting. I'd brought along rolls of foam rubber, but they didn't do any good. I tried kneeling but the open wounds on my knees were too painful. In addition, owing to my poor circulation, my thigh cramps grew steadily worse. God almighty, how my legs hurt! I couldn't manage to be comfortable in any position. I would have given anything to be able to sleep a little. The edges of the lockers directly below me dug into my ribs. It felt as though I was stretched out on rocky ground and somebody was rolling me over and over. My bruises felt like third–degree

---

*The capital of the large French island of New Caledonia in the South Pacific, 650 miles from Australia.

burns. I cried tears of fatigue constantly. It was like the infamous method of torture that involves denying the prisoner any rest. There can be nothing worse; exhaustion can drive you to the brink of insanity. Any ocean rower could give up the crossing just for one night's sleep. *Pilot* never stopped her sickening elevator-gone-wild movement, rising upward on a wave crest, then plunging down into the trough. The usual exhausting din resounded in my ears. Once more, I imagined being somewhere else, a beach of fine sand, in the sun — yes, nice and warm — some place where I could finally get a little rest. I focused on a few breathing exercises, trying to relax a bit. It was 11 P.M. when I began dozing off, wrapped up in dreams of vacations in the islands. I tried to forget my predicament. I stopped thinking about the immense ocean, the vicious storm, the noise that left me shaking like a frightened child. I simply wasn't here anymore; it had all been just a nightmare.

I slept for a few minutes — too few — and now my radar detector jolted me awake with its insistent beeping, and grim reality came flooding back. I scrambled out of the spot where I'd managed to create some semblance of warmth. I lighted a cabin lamp to alleviate my anxiety. It had started to rain — undoubtedly, the front of the depression coming through. I was shaking violently at this point. The intensity of the alarm made my ears ring. And the warning was steady, meaning that the freighter couldn't be very far away. I glanced all around from my Plexiglas bubble but saw no running lights anywhere. The seas were too high, hiding the stranger from view. I heard the waves coming, one after the other, but couldn't see them. There was no getting around it — I had to go topside. Plucking up my courage, I grabbed my safety harness/lifeline and my watch coat and struggled into them. I hated getting dressed in the cabin. It was so cramped that I usually bumped myself several times. But it was pouring, so I had no other choice. Once I'd gotten all my gear on, I listened to the roar of the waves. I measured the risks of showing myself on deck; those risks, always high at night, were especially high in rough weather. Let's go, over the top with you, my Active Echo radar seemed to bark at me. What's crucial is making sure not to go topside at the wrong moment — and not to forget the golden rule: One hand for the ship, one hand for yourself. Opening the hatch, I clutched my lifeline to clip it in the cockpit and crawled out without losing a second. *Pilot* was bouncing around, lurching drunkenly. So I wouldn't fall overboard, I clung to the two handrails — one to port, the other to starboard. I turned my head and nearly choked when I saw the huge ship emerging from the seas; I could make out two white lights — one up forward and another on her stern. The red light on her starboard side told me she meant to cut across my bow. Then I lost sight of her in the seas and was terrified that she was going to reappear — *right alongside me.* Then I saw her again. The ship was closing the gap between us; fortunately, I was so much slower that she would be gone before our courses intersected. In situations like these, time seems to stand still. What if the ship changed course? What if the wind drove *Pilot* right into her? If only ships knew that we were there! Unfortunately, it is impossible to warn all those merchant vessels. And, then, *Pilot* being as small as she is, the freighters would never spot me — even if they were looking. By now, the huge ship had gone on her way. With each passing second, I began to breathe more easily.

I realized then that, on top of being half-frozen, I was now also soaked to the skin. And, this time, there was no certainty I could warm up. But I felt relieved all the same. I quickly ducked into the cabin and stripped off my wet clothes. Despite all my precautions, I couldn't help getting water over everything — much to my annoyance. I lay my watch coat down in a spot where it would drip only on the cabin sole and, once more, quickly grabbed my (partially dry) eiderdown quilt.

On other nights, this scenario could be reenacted as many as three or four times. Other times, I just didn't go topside at all; quite simply, I was too tired. Despite the risk, despite my fear of dying, I sometimes felt so weary that nothing seemed to matter anymore; only sleep mattered, a few hours' sleep. Fortunately, such grim thoughts didn't last long; each time, I managed to regain my incredible will to live, to survive. I kept telling myself that it was only a question of time and that, sooner or later, I would be free of my prison.

The days passed. The sea grew less agitated. The skies cleared and this raised my spirits. It made me think about all those people back home who were going away on their summer vacations without a care in the world. The sun peeked out and a multitude of small, blue-tinged clouds crackled the sky, reminding me of the crazed porcelain of Grandmother's worn old coffee cup. I powered up my GPS and realized that, a few seconds before, I had actually done it — I'd scaled the wall. No, wall isn't right, *the mountain.* My little *Pilot* and I were at the line that marked the halfway point!

I had mixed feelings about this event. For one thing, I remembered that first week at sea, those harrowing days when, trembling with cold, my palms blistered, I struggled to get the Newfoundland coast to slip beneath the horizon. The middle of the Atlantic had then been so far off it seemed beyond my reach. Then I was groping through fog and there was nothing to suggest I would ever find my way out of it. But, on the Grand Banks, too, the hours, the days dragged by, seemingly more and more slowly, and my palms gradually became calloused. I crossed off the weeks on my calendar, one after the other. I would glare defiantly at the month of September, which seemed to heckle me. Those long days hardened my body and, stroke after stroke, strengthened my resolve never to give up.

Waking up on the morning of August 5, at longitude 31 degrees west, I was struck by the magnitude of being alone over a thousand miles from my point of departure, and the task ahead — it would take many, many days of rowing to reach the Britanny Peninsula in France. Out here, in Mid-Atlantic, a rower had better not need anything urgently; I kept my fingers crossed that I wouldn't have any problems with my health. By the time some vessel made a detour to come for me, plus the time needed to get me ashore, more than a week could go by. If I came down with acute appendicitis, I'm not sure I could even hold out a week. Paradoxically, with this kind of crossing, you can only give up when everything is going well and you have lots of time. While my friends from the Rescue Center at Gris Nez* could try to locate the ship nearest me and ask them to go out of their way to help me, there was no guarantee any freighter would be in my neck of the woods. Four or five days . . . that's kind of a long wait when you've got a serious problem. And anyway, if the sea is rough, any rescuing ship might not be able to come alongside my boat to get me off without smashing us to smithereens.

I often thought about my appendix, which I'd never bothered to have removed. Naturally, lots of other problems can arise: malfunctioning equipment, running out of provisions, springing a leak. I wouldn't take bets on my chances of surviving any of those problems. But when it came to my appendix, I did have the choice. Before my departure, I decided against having surgery and made the trip, appendix intact. Dr. Chauve, who helped me select the medical equipment to keep onboard, made me feel better about my decision. He explained that the risks of post-operative complications were often more serious than those of the inflamed appendix itself. And by then I would have run out of time. Deep down, I must admit, I kicked myself for making that decision. I swept this health worry under the rug so I could savor the pleasure of being where I was now.

As I had promised, I dug out the glass bottle I'd brought along and wrote a message, adding the line from Joseph Conrad that you read at the beginning of this book: *"To follow the dream, and again to follow the dream — and so — always — usque ad finem."* I set the bottle down in the water and watched it as we drifted apart. It contained much more than a slip of paper.

---

*On the English Channel near Calais.

The bottle recorded the date, August 5, 2003; a dream that was coming true; the gorgeous day filled with sunshine; and then, too, my twenty-five years; my round and voluminous handwriting style at the time; my fierce will to get here — even if it meant moving mountains. The bottle represented a magic moment, but it was also setting out on a voyage of its own. I kept watching it as it bobbed on the surface of the water, seeking the shore on which it would one day land. I wondered if anyone would ever read the message. It's strange, but I really felt, releasing that bottle, that I had made time stand still. It wasn't a photo; better yet, it combined smells, colors, fingerprints, and even sweat. I hoped it would take the longest possible time and travel the farthest possible distance before being found. And isn't this the ultimate goal of a message in a bottle? To resist the passage of time and be found only when worn by the surf? The message inside would be yellowed by the sun, faded by the dampness, half illegible — but then, it might just bring this marvelous day back to life.

Coming out of my reverie, I looked first behind and then in front of me. Just to think, I'd come this far by the muscles in my arms! I had trouble believing it.

Standing in the cockpit, staring at the horizon, I held my breath, trying not to spoil that extraordinary moment. The sea gleamed like a silvery tablecloth pleated by a gentle breeze. The sun appeared, a complete disk, and warmed my shoulders. Everything was blue, as if that were the only color left in the world. The horizon melted into the sky. Under my feet, *Pilot* danced in a gentle rhythm. It was such a grand moment that I dared not utter a word. Often, over the cellular phone, people asked me whether I sang or screamed when I was alone. Space at sea is so vast that some people may be tempted — just once and only once — to let out a scream from the depths of their being. For liberating oneself, perhaps for feeling alive and, certainly, also for doing what is prohibited. As for me, that wasn't at all the case — I didn't feel this need. Quite the contrary. I wanted to be discreet, delicate; I wanted to be as close as I possibly could to nature and draw still closer. Even when I spoke aloud to myself, I did it in a whisper, very gently. Or when I encouraged my boat, I whispered, very softly, so as not to upset my fascinating natural surroundings, so as not to dispel the magnetism enveloping me at that moment. It was magical; I had the impression of being inside a soap bubble, light and variegated. I didn't want to risk bursting its fragile walls. I didn't want to impose myself. Curiously, I remained a bit superstitious. The sea was unforgiving; it would not be in my best interest to wake the superhuman force slumbering beneath me. Nothing was gained and it was better to be discreet. It was as if I was tiptoeing on the back of a sleeping leviathan that would soon wake up — it was inevitable. But the longer he slept the better. So I savored each moment with delight, imbuing myself with the serenity of the elements as you might with a delicious perfume you didn't want to forget. The rewards were wonderful. I forgot about my hands, the boils that blossomed on my salt-weakened skin, my scars. The frightful experiences of stormy nights were erased from my mind; everything was beautiful. I filled my lungs until I didn't know where to put all that good air; the oxygen refreshed me enough that I even went up and sat on the little forward deck. Freedom smelled good. My outer shell, almost indispensable in our modern life in society, had grown softer week after week, and today I had the feeling it had disappeared completely. I really felt free. Of course, what I had accomplished was a physical exploit, a voyage first and foremost. True freedom is choosing to go beyond yourself, pushing yourself to the limits, struggling to live out the dream in the depths of your soul; finally, that freedom is having an extraordinary feeling of fulfillment. If I succeeded, I would never say, "I beat the sea." You can't *beat* the sea. Mariners become humble, and then the sea may — or may not — allow them through. I don't have the mind-set of a great sports figure; rather, I am a woman adventurer, if I may say so. Of course, the path I took wasn't the easiest, but this was exactly what made it so fabulous. In my opinion, that's how we make ourselves stronger and better — by facing difficulty, adversity, and transcending ourselves. Only in such extreme ventures can we have such intense emotions. These come from so far away that they thrill every fiber in your body like a current of electricity.

I experienced this moment of absolute joy early in August. I had never felt anything so strongly before. All the hardships I'd encountered up until then merely served to heighten that pleasure. Never had I felt the life force seething within me as it did now.

Naturally, this couldn't last too long. *Pilot* was still tiny, the distance to be covered enormous. The fear in the pit of my stomach wasn't going to die, it would only subside for a while. It was simply a temporary respite, a chance to get my strength back. I gobbled it up. But the world didn't end there. Life went on and I had to return to my oars.

Atmospheric conditions improved. I had to grab this opportunity to make progress. While moving back and forth on the sliding seat, I pondered that magical moment. Yes, it was already in the past. I wondered why the god of the sea had chosen to keep me in the palm of his hand. Why hadn't he put me back on the beach empty-handed, as many people had predicted? Yet, from Day One, Neptune had unquestionably been the boss. He made the rules: I just had to look humble, put up with all his moods, take all of his guff, and console myself with the thought he couldn't stay angry forever. Rather than get angry with him, I just figured he was sick — subject to uncontrollable seizures or migraine headaches that drove him crazy. And I certainly must have done the right thing not standing up to the god of the sea; after all, he had been putting up with me since June 13. He'd held open a narrow little path for me, closing his eyes to my rather short arms . . . and the fact that I "was a girl," as a reporter once put it. Today he gave me a gift of inestimable value. I had only one wish: that I might carry this treasure always and, opening it from time to time, share it with you. And to think it all started with a simple dream. . . . But, as Walt Disney once said, "For a plan to become a reality, it must first be dreamed."

It was always the same old refrain. The days went by, one after another, interminably. And the same held true for the gales: they struck one after another. We had come to the end of August and I was doing my last "live" broadcast with media personality, Laurent Cabrol, on a Sunday morning. Summer was ending; I was gradually getting closer to Europe. "Just a quarter of the run to go," friends kept telling me. "You're almost there. Don't get discouraged." I received dozens of e-mails full of encouragement. Mother would read them and tell me about them when I phoned. It was great to know that people were following my progress on a daily basis. In a way, I was rowing for them. Yes, deep down, there was a desire to set an example and not let those people down. If I could just face this challenge. . . . I hoped it would lend courage to those who didn't dare pursue their dreams, those afraid they might not succeed. I received very touching letters from people who were lonely, in distress, or for whom life had lost all its flavor. If only I could bring them proof that we can do anything we set out to do. That we can make our dreams come true if only we work at it; that it's always worth trying; that we are capable of great things; and that we use only a fraction of our potential. Within us, we all have immeasurable strength and we need only find it. Deep inside me, these ideas resonated forcefully. If I could manage to share what I'd discovered, what I felt out here on the sea each day, then my transatlantic crossing would not have been in vain. For that reason alone I wouldn't give up.

The coast of Europe rapidly drew closer. I was moving ahead at a good clip and had no technical breakdowns. All things considered, I would be arriving in time for my birthday in early September and for the birth of Yann's daughter. My family and friends had already made plans for my arrival; I half expected them to ask me what time I'd cross the finish line on the Brittany peninsula. I was very impatient! Liberation was at hand. I missed dry land terribly. Ten more days and I'd be on it. I became more and more excited. The wind was starting to rise, but my meteorological bureau friends announced that it wouldn't be too bad — 20–25 knots at most. Rough weather, but nothing to get really worked up about — not with all I'd already been through. . . .

The future would prove to be something quite different.

Part 3

Contrary Winds

7

Thirty-Six Hours in a Gale — Clouds of Plankton — Tracy Chapman

WATER WAS TRICKLING IN EVERYWHERE. Rivulets ran all over the cabin and ceiling, drops landing on my face. Everything, from eiderdown quilt to polar fleece jacket to cellular phone and GPS — even my body — was all salty. It was sticky, it had a stale, musty smell . . . there was no more air.

Again, I was penned up in my little cabin, sheltered from the ocean raging out on deck. The situation was getting worse by the hour. I had never seen the seas build up so fast before. The wind was blowing harder and harder, reaching fifty knots in gusts, wreaking havoc in its path. The flags secured to the jackstay chattered like machine guns, fluttering and snapping, until I thought they would tear apart. The waves at first were short and steep, then took on gargantuan proportions, measuring thirty feet high and breaking with such force that I dared not look at them from the Plexiglas bubble. At a height of three-story buildings, they rushed my tiny boat, striking from behind with a growl that was truly terrifying. While each part of my body trembled, I clenched my teeth. I was on the verge of a panic attack.

At this point, I understood the full meaning of the expression "to die of fright." In the grip of anxiety, my nerves frayed, I clawed at my own flesh, digging my nails into my arms and face — without realizing what I was doing. My body no longer obeyed me. I still shudder at the memory of this, the worst moment of my life.

The breaking waves submerged my craft; capsize followed capsize, one right after another, not giving me a second to recover. Everything broke in the cabin: the overhead dome light disintegrated, fragments of the bulb scattered everywhere; a locker burst open, spewing its contents. I hung on with all my might. My knee had struck the edge of my bunk, and now I couldn't move my leg. I yelled out in pain and despair. I couldn't breathe, as there was no more air in the cabin. Coughing, spitting, I was completely exhausted, totally dehydrated. For thirty-six hours I'd had nothing to eat, nothing to drink; I hadn't closed my eyes for a second. My wrist was sprained, and I was now unable to use that hand to hold on with. In addition, I suspected I had two cracked ribs. I was going to die. I didn't want to die. I was only twenty-five years old, and I wanted children. I hadn't come out here to die. No, please let me live. I wanted to see the sun come up again. Uncontrollable fear gripped me; I was battered from head to foot; I even lacked the strength to crack the hatch for a breath of air. Topside, the ocean raged, the wind howling its fury. The clouds were jet-black, so dense and so vast that I couldn't tell if it was day or night. Wedging myself in the cabin as best

I could, I phoned land to get meteorological information. A gloomy voice replied that I would still have gale-force winds for another twenty-four hours, the depression having stalled around me. I could do nothing but wait — wait the twenty-four interminable hours until the gale began to subside.

I couldn't believe what I'd heard. Losing my temper, I shouted: "That's impossible. I tell you I can't hold out. *Pilot* is going to break apart. This boat can't withstand this kind of sea and wind that long."

Just then an enormous breaking wave engulfed the tiny craft and we lost all ship-to-shore contact.

My boat shuddered, groaning from stem to stern, and I began to tremble even harder. That rogue wave had carried away everything in its path: my sliding seat had literally been torn from its moorings. Nothing remained in the cockpit. The next thing to go would surely be the Plexiglas dome in the cabin roof. God, please let that hold. I quickly stowed the phone to save it from the wave impacts and the water sloshing around the cabin. I moved the maximum amount of weight aft so that the boat would not broach — that is, go broadside — to the oncoming waves. Rising on the crests of mountainous seas, the boat then took a roller-coaster ride down their steep faces, while I could see the valley floor waiting beneath us. I was convinced that, falling so far and slamming that hard into the trough, she would never ride up again.

At such times, the noise level inside the cabin was enough to drive anyone mad. I saw myself drowning: the boat would be filled with water in a few minutes. With each new wave, I feared that she would not come back up to the surface. I was totally helpless. It was dark; the water was cold; I had the taste of death in my mouth. I prayed that the gale wouldn't last much longer but couldn't push the succession of grim thoughts from my mind. Would it take one minute or two for my lungs to fill with water? I longed for some whiskey to help me forget, to calm me, so that I wouldn't so clearly see death coming. I thought of those I loved, of the thousand plans I had for the future, of the babies I talked about constantly. I wondered how I could ever have complained about the little irritations of everyday life, how I — like everyone — whined about getting up early in the morning, about having pain in my feet. And why had I been so timid about trying my luck to find a sponsor? I thought of all those things that had seemed so hard during the preparations for my crossing and that seemed so useless now. I prayed to all the gods: The Almighty, Neptune, Poseidon, Triton. I promised that if they let me live to see another day and let me glimpse the sea again the way it was just thirty-six hours earlier, I would be the nicest, the most patient of women. I'd never again complain about all those trifles that worry us or put us in a bad mood. If I could only get through this gale, things would change. If I could get out of this jam, I would love the whole world. I said all these things aloud to calm myself. Once more — as I did whenever the situation became unbearable — I yearned for somebody to be with me. The solitude was terrifying. I felt so utterly alone in the face of death. The fear of dying when you are far from your loved ones, far from land, forgotten on that immense ocean — is something beyond description. Yet, more than a thousand miles away, my family, friends, hundreds of Internet pals, were suffering with me. At home, I knew my mother would be like a zombie; nobody spoke to each other. They knew the sea and understood that nothing could be done for me. It was impossible to send help — no vessel could have approached me in a storm like this. There was nothing to do but wait. My family slept in one-hour shifts, taking turns standing by the phone. We would speak briefly, just for a second, and I'd give them the number of new capsizes: one, two . . . biting their nails, keeping their fingers crossed, lighting candles, they stopped at nothing and clutched at any straw to boost their morale and mine. Messages of support poured into my Web site — there was a large "family" following my adventure.

That night of August 27 was the worst of my voyage: seventeen capsizes, all kinds of damage to *Pilot*. Long after this gale and sometimes even now, I wake up crying, thinking about it. Gérard d'Aboville likens capsizes to automobile accidents, but with this difference: in the case of a car, the whole thing lasts only a few seconds, but, in a gale, the horror drags on hour after hour. A capsize is a perpetual accident that can happen over and over again. It marks you for life. Those fearful scenes will continue to haunt me.

Inside the cabin, everything had been thrown upside down. It was in a state beyond recognition. The only thing that remained in its place was the bright red clown nose my father had given me before I sailed. I never took my eyes off it; that alone represented my hope of reaching land — and of smiling again. This struggle for life, with the enormous physical and mental strain it entailed, had exhausted me. I was quite incapable of reaching the hatch to crack it enough to let in some air. My muscles had been so battered that, now, every move caused me pain. I was using the very last scrap of energy that remained within me to weather the storm. Throughout those thirty-six hours in hell, I nonetheless continued to steer with my foot, thereby preventing a number of capsizes by helping *Pilot* to go *with* the waves. During this battle, I often glanced at my watch: Time seemed to stand still, yet the hands of my watch had gone full circle more than twice in the storm.

About noon, the front of the depression passed and the sea began to flatten: twenty-seven-foot waves, then twenty-four-foot waves, then twenty-one-foot waves. The sky underwent a transformation, going from black to dark gray; the tired monster was gradually moving away. I couldn't believe *Pilot* and I had come through it. I was still terribly anxious, fearful that the sea would build up again, that it was just playing a trick on us. The ocean might come at my tiny craft again — only this time, with even more force. But the wind started to drop off — well, not all at once. All day long, that night, and the following day, I stayed in the cabin, a prisoner. I had to wait for the seas to calm more before I could set foot on deck. Little by little, I regained my composure and began trying to create a semblance of order in my cage. After bailing out the seawater, I tried to rinse out a few articles in fresh water. Then I bandaged my wrist, coating it with skin cream first. I fixed myself a bite to eat and, believe me, that postgale, freeze-dried meal was a treat. Sheer joy!

If there is anything such an experience as mine leaves you with, it's the realization of how fragile our lives are. Life, all too often taken for granted, is seldom recognized at its true value. We fail to perceive its ephemeral side. And I had ample time to think this one over. The new life bestowed on me today is priceless. I'm going to cherish it. Again, my advice is: Get closer to your feelings and grab the object of your desire as fast as you can. It's a terrible feeling when it slips through your fingers.

Through those long hours, those entire days and nights of waiting, memories of my childhood at sea came to mind. Of course, these had nothing to do with the dreadful moments I was living through. I remembered a beautiful warm day. My two brothers and I were living a totally carefree life. We were fed on the day's catch from my father's underwater spear fishing; as well, we ate fried green bananas or cooked yams. We had no need of more than that; every afternoon we swam and played. We were free and happy. The sea was unquestionably the embodiment of that happiness. My love of the ocean remains deep within me. As a little girl, I loved to keep salt water in my mouth, just for fun. Who knows? Maybe my blood is saltier than that of other people's. But one thing is sure: The ocean draws me like a magnet. As for its fury, I tried to understand it. I was convinced that it wasn't the ocean's fault; it was just experiencing pressure changes. At no time did I feel that we were locked in battle, one against the other. No, I submitted, I endured, I clung to the hope of surviving, begging for rest. I am convinced that the god of the sea was doing his best to spare my life. He nonetheless frightened the wits out of me — that's undeniable. He had scared me so badly this time that now, even when the waves were beginning to diminish in height, I still dared not set foot on deck. For that matter, I scarcely ventured to look through the Plexiglas shield. I feared that the gale would be unleashed all over again, that the weather reports would be proved wrong again. But at some point I'd have to go on deck. It was essential that I overcome my fear.

I remember learning to ride a horse. Whenever I fell — which happened with some regularity — my instructor wouldn't tolerate so much as a second's hesitation. Even before I had time to collect my wits, he was there, forcing me back into the saddle. Here, it was somewhat the same. I knew that I had to force myself to fight. My hatch was ajar and I pushed it open. It had never seemed so heavy.

Pain shot through my knee as I wormed my way through the tiny exit and crawled into the cockpit. A wave had shorn off the sliding seat, so there was lots more room than usual. I slowly managed to pull myself up, feeling quite dizzy. I might well have a pinched nerve in my spine; at any rate, straightening my back felt like trying to unroll rusty iron wire. I must have looked a fright. In that gale, I'd probably lost ten or twelve pounds. Being weak in the knees, I couldn't manage to stay on my feet for very long. I sat down, leaning my back against the forward hatch. The seas still ran about four or five feet high. Like watchdogs, they barked and growled around *Pilot*. I winced at the sight of them — they looked as if they'd soon bite again.

Darkness fell. The night sky was clear, so I could watch the stars come out, one after the other. There was a full moon that night, and the stars twinkled. I'd never expected to see stars again. And then, without so much as a "by your leave," the sea changed into a river of diamonds. Layers of phosphorescent plankton, struck by the moonbeams, sparkled. Deeply moved by this magical spectacle of the Atlantic, I felt a gust of warmth envelope me.

My mind was clear now; the elements had calmed, the nightmare had ended, and I was still alive. I made my peace with the ocean; words weren't strong enough to express my deep gratitude. I'd been so sure that I was going to die, that I would never see the end of those hellish thirty-six hours. Riding out this storm had been traumatic, but I'd been allowed to live and, as far as I was concerned, that was all that mattered. I only hoped that I would never forget, never let that struggle fade from my memory, that I wouldn't forget the joy of that evening, the promises I'd made.

I hoped I would always remember that this marvelous thing we call life can be lost in a second. I had been sliding down the razor's edge and, at last, I could breathe. The ocean had decided to keep me, whereas the other two solo rowers (a Ukrainian and a Frenchman) who had set out around the same time as me from North America had been forced to give up owing to the particularly capricious weather that year. I wondered what I owed this luck to. I had held out mentally because I'd refused to let myself be caught in the trap of my own fear, of my own suffering. My fate could easily have gone one way or the other, but it went my way. Feeling reborn, I savored that night with delight. I was alone at sea, but *I was there* and so proud of it.

Late that night, I returned to the cabin where I promptly fell into a deep sleep. Waking up refreshed the following morning, I had much to do. But before facing the day's chores, I took out my little radio and began trying its frequency knob in hopes of catching a musical air wave on the wing. I was, after all, getting closer to the coast of Europe. I got some highly unpleasant static, and after a few minutes I was about to give up when a voice came on that was warm, melodious, and a bit husky. I heard only a few notes, a few murmured words, but it was enough to recognize the Tracy Chapman song I'd listened to in October, the day I'd decided to "take the plunge," when I'd made that first down payment on my boat. The coincidence astounded me. Then I lost the station, a Spanish voice replacing Tracy Chapman before fading out in its turn. With a light heart, I tackled my work: I jury-rigged a seat to replace the sliding one that the storm had carried away. Because of my knee injury, I had to get used to rowing using only my upper body. Then I worked out a good technique for holding my oars so as to favor my badly sprained wrist; for this, I kept my grip as loose as possible, so that my fingers scarcely rested on the oars. And my wrist got better. But during this whole time, that same bit of music kept running through my mind. I'd passed my test and had emerged the stronger for it. I didn't look at the ocean in the same way anymore. I would never again be that happy-go-lucky girl or be quite so innocent. But the ocean had allowed me to go on breathing and, for that, we would remain bound forever.

8

Desalinator Breakdown — Easterly Winds — *Sill* — Sharks and Barnacles

WHEN THINGS GO WRONG, they really go wrong. It was the end of August and I'd missed the birth of my niece, Anya Fontenoy. They told me that Yann and Gipsy were in seventh heaven. I was furious at not being with them. They told me the baby had a full head of hair and that she hardly ever cried. Apparently Mother made the wish that the new baby become "as strong as Maud!"

Winds from the north had shoved me far south of what my course should have been, so that now I was on the same latitude as Spain or Portugal — instead of France, and even less so of my intended landfall on the Brittany Peninsula. If that weren't enough, my desalinator went on the blink. Its motor ran nicely enough but not a drop of fresh water came out. This machine was mounted in a well to starboard, under the cockpit — where it was practically inaccessible. I immediately whipped out the manual. I read it over and over, reciting the instructions as I'd already done before starting my voyage, but for the life of me I couldn't figure out what the trouble was. The water appeared to be getting through, the motor was running and activating the pump piston; nevertheless, only concentrated salt water came out and not a drop of potable water. I knew that I had a spare desalinator: the identical machine, only hand-operated. This reserve device was stowed in a locker way up forward. I was in no hurry to pull it out of its hiding place, preferring to repair the battery-operated one. Using the satellite telephone, I managed to reach my shore-based team, who quickly sought information from the manufacturer and the architect — in vain. Nobody could understand what the problem was. What if you change the filter? All right, I'll change it. Still nothing. That couldn't have been the problem. Then they told me I'd have to drain the biocide completely. Having little choice in the matter, I did their bidding, which was no cinch down in that tiny well of a work space. *Pilot* wouldn't stop bouncing us around and it was all I could do to keep a tight grip on my buckets of anti-bacterial solution. This activity robbed me of several precious hours that I would have preferred devoting to my oars, making up the time I'd lost that week. It was getting late into the season and I really wanted to be out of harm's way.

After two days of trying everything, I decided to go for my reserve desalinator. Somehow I managed to wriggle into the claustrophobic forward cabin and haul out my spare machine. Now, if only this one worked! But with the desalinator unpacked, the task no longer seemed as easy as I'd imagined. For one thing, the machine was heavy and thus hard to move. Then, one hose had to be long enough to reach over the side to pump seawater; next, the fresh water had to be collected in a clean receptacle; last, I couldn't permit a mixture of wastewater and salt to slosh around the cabin and get into my boots. I tried every possible position, but to no avail: Absolutely nothing could keep the machine from sliding. Three times in a row it failed to process the water. I thought I was going to blow a gasket myself. I had to get this damned thing fixed!

Because I was running low on water, I hadn't dipped into my reserves in the two previous days. But even imposing strict rationing on my freshwater consumption, I still used about a gallon a day. I sat down to think the situation out. I had a headache and, to top it off, I was hungry. I needed to find a solution before making myself a freeze-dried meal.

For several weeks, I had been cutting back on food: The days were passing and that European coast was still awfully far away. The water shortage was only aggravating my difficulties since no water meant no food — I couldn't rehydrate my freeze-dried dishes. So I had to fasten that machine to something. I looked around for a good spot where I could activate its lever with maximum force. Finally, it dawned on me: Secure the desalinator to one of the forward handrails. Of course, it was a makeshift solution and a bit shaky, but I'd be reaching land before too long. (At least I sure hoped so.) I brought out two or three lengths of rope and securely lashed the machine to the forward deck. Next, I placed a jerry can of seawater in the cockpit because *Pilot* had too much forward freeboard for the hose to reach into the ocean. I then prepared another jerry can for the fresh water I would collect. As for the salt-laden wastewater, it would run the length of the hull. It was simple. Everything was ready, so I started the tests. The pump lever was still hard to activate, but at least I could use both hands on it. This seemed to work. I pumped for ten minutes or so before tasting the water to make sure all the biocide had been eliminated. This is a toxic substance and I had no intention of getting sick at this point. I stopped pumping and put the hose to my lips. It only came out drop by drop, but the main thing was I could drink the stuff. So everything was all right; true, the water was tasteless, odorless, totally demineralized. But that was exactly what I'd expected. The machine worked. I went on pumping long into the night in order to build up a sufficient supply. Because of the position I had to work in, I wouldn't be able to use the machine during a storm. I had to pump for three-quarters of an hour to produce two quarts of water. At that rate, I wouldn't be taking many baths.

My jury-rigged desalinator certainly didn't last very long. Two weeks later, a new catastrophe struck. The pump handle had just broken off in my hands. This time I knew the situation was really dangerous and naturally, I felt terribly thirsty all of a sudden. I sat there with my head in my hands, trying to absorb the sledgehammer blow I'd just taken from this discovery. It seldom rained in this part of the North Atlantic and I had a total water reserve of exactly three gallons. I started getting chest pains. A lot of questions involving dying of thrist were running through my mind. I tried to get hold of myself. I knew people just didn't *die* like that overnight. Maybe they didn't die suddenly, but I could be forced to give up the crossing as a result of this unforeseen setback. And I was so near the end.

I couldn't stand it when anyone asked me for my estimated date of arrival. I kept telling reporters I didn't have a clue. It depended on a zillion things and most were out of my control. I was over three hundred nautical miles (around six hundred kilometers) from the coast, with no means of making fresh water. Those congratulatory messages telling me that I'd done it, that it was all over, really drove me crazy. I felt like screaming out, "No, it isn't!" Nothing was all over. Victory could easily go one way or the other. I more than anyone wanted to believe I'd done it, that it *was* all over. I wanted desperately to see my loved ones, to be finished with the crossing. All those Internet messages only twisted the knife in the wound. Deep down, we love to think we've done it; we keep on fantasizing about that finish line. It was the old "pride goeth before a fall." I'd been tumbled, been humbled. What was I supposed to do without water? I tried to clear this flood of dismal thinking from my brain. I had to come up with an answer. Quite simply, I had to find out what went wrong with the first desalinator.

That marked the start of what I might term a rotten week. Since it was impossible to predict how long the repairs would take, I made plans to economize with my scant supply of fresh water. Gérard d'Aboville managed to put me in touch with Alain Bombard, whom I'd met before setting out. Famous for his solo ocean crossings, Bombard advised me to replace one-third of my daily ration with seawater — which I began doing immediately. Of course, this notion is highly controversial; it can lead to kidney failure, the body not being designed to distill that much salt. Everybody started to gather information and messages poured in. My onshore team contacted specialists like Dominique Jan, a surgeon friend in New York. He discussed the matter with his department, and the other doctors were adamant: I might as well drink my own urine than drink seawater. I knew that, in many Indian tribes, urine is commonly used as a preventive medicine. The stuff is full of antibodies, I grant you. That does give it many therapeutic qualities, but still . . . !

The crossing had taken an unexpected turn. I had gone through the survival-at-sea stage and now the risk of dehydration was stalking me. I forced myself to smile about my situation. Giving way to depression or going into a panic wouldn't do much to help.

So, for a week, I was forced to alternate drinking seawater and my own urine. Having so little fresh water, I further restricted my intake of food. This period was the worst, from a physical standpoint. I was losing weight and, virtually, all my strength. I suffered repeated dizzy spells and endless migraine headaches. The great quantity of salt I took in gave me stomachaches. I felt a terrible weight in my belly. I wondered how Alain Bombard had managed to get through it. If, at least, like him, I had caught fish, I could have extracted a small quantity of liquid from them. But they refused to bite at my line. The first signs of thirst had begun to make themselves felt and my diet — already lean — became downright starvation rations. One night, I was so hungry that, despite being bone-tired, I couldn't fall asleep. Finally, at 3 A.M., I got up and rehydrated something to eat. After all, I needed the strength to be able to go on rowing.

Drawing on the last reserves of my strength, I somehow found the energy to continue each day, to move ahead toward

my salvation. If only it would rain! At times some panel of
sky took on a tallowy hue and I thought I was going to be
able to collect a gallon or so of water. As soon as the droplets
began to fall, I stopped what I was doing. I got out my cook-
ing pots and stretched a large plastic bag across the cockpit.
And, just at that point, the rain would always stop. My friends
joked that I must have "invented" a tarpaulin that made the
rain stop, and they advised me to have it patented right away.
Once more, I preferred to laugh about it. But the situation
was growing worse with each passing day; hunger kept me
from sleeping and it obsessed me. I was experiencing unbearable stomach pangs. I even went around with a teaspoon trying to scoop up a few drops of water in the cockpit. I never
thought it would come to this, but I remained hopeful; I went
on studying my manual for repairing the battery-operated
desalinator. First, I had to drag the machine out of the compartment where it was kept. And that was no mean task. I
needed to smash the bulkhead before I could even try to extract the beast, weighing some thirty-three pounds (fifteen
kilos). Then, squatting in my cabin, thoroughly nauseated, I
struggled while the ocean went on undulating and *Pilot* rolled
and pitched tirelessly. The waves were running a good nine
feet high — not exactly conducive to performing repair work
below decks. Ever since my departure, I'd been in dread of
having to fix anything afloat. Even back on land, I'd had
trouble understanding the desalinator's reverse osmosis system
but, now, all alone in the cabin, I had a hunch it was really out
to get me. With a vomit bucket on one side and the machine
on the other, I donned my thinking cap. I looked at the
gadget from every angle, turning it first this way, then that,

trying to establish some kind of connection between the actual machine and the diagrams in the damned instruction booklet. At last, I decided to take my chances. After two hours of disassembly and reassembly, I finally shoved the blasted thing back into its compartment, saying aloud, "If only it would work!" Anyway, if it still didn't work, one thing would be certain — that I'd tried my level best to do the impossible. For me, that was everything. This whole adventure was designed to enable me to surpass myself, to forget all my long-held (and limiting) beliefs, to learn to manage on my own. My mind turned the desalinator problem into a lesson about life; it became a hurdle to overcome with regard to my own doubts. I had to learn to have confidence in myself. How come girls didn't know how to fix things? Generally, when something of the kind needed doing around our home, my parents sent for the boys, my two brothers. And I would fight to go with them, to watch, to have the right to get my hands dirty. But now I imagined they were there to help me. I switched the machine on, and its motor kicked over. I hovered anxiously around the fresh water outlet, but nothing came out. I knew I had to wait. "Be patient, Maud," *Pilot* seemed to whisper. Another few minutes and — presto! — clear water started dripping into my bottle. Yippee! I'd done it. I felt like dancing, singing. I'd gotten the desalinator to work again. What a victory! I made a quart of water and began heating it to rehydrate some spaghetti Bolognese — a real treat.

That night was calmer and I no longer had to consider giving up my voyage on account of technical problems. Whew, what a relief! Time was going by, and my crossing continued.

On September 7, I celebrated my birthday alone at

sea — with no chocolate layer cake. I was twenty-six now. A gale sprang up and I capsized twice that night.

A few days later, some ideal weather kept me excited about the prospect of a beautiful sunset. I wasn't disappointed when evening came — it was gorgeous. The sea around us had a pink hue. That gave it a new look, a tender and sweet mixture — feminine, even. The sun turned crimson on meeting the sea. From time to time, it hid behind the clouds, which were at once fringed with fire. The spectacle was moving: After each bout of rough weather, the ocean always sought to console me. The following day, I dedicated my logbook entry to my mother. I could still hear the words she had whispered to me on the day I left Paris. It was a passage from French singer-songwriter Léo Ferré:

> *With time we forget the voices*
> *That told us quietly in the words of poor folk:*
> *Don't come back too late, most of all, don't get a chill.*

Mother's words were like a tiny bell shaken by *Pilot*'s motion; I remembered the tears she could no longer keep in before I embarked, her distress when I said good-bye, the promise that I made to be careful, to return safe and sound to her before winter. Time was dragging by so slowly.

A few days later, I met Roland Jourdain, who was sailing the sixty-foot *Sill* with his British teammate. We both worked with the same meteorologist, and Roland had heard that my boat wasn't far from his. And since his course would take him near my position, he insisted on dropping off a jerry can of water in case my desalinator was up to its old tricks again. I found comfort in this solidarity among sailors. I waited for him all day, delighted at having a visit. This would be my first human contact after three and a half months of solitude, except for my early encounter with the trawler a few days into my voyage. Unfortunately, the weather prevented Roland from actually coming alongside for a chat: The wind started blowing so hard that my boat became unmanageable. I saw him coming over the horizon: first, the tip of his mast and then the whole sail. Finally, I could see the brilliant red hull. *Sill* came up as proudly as a knight. I couldn't wait to see Roland. He came as close as possible to *Pilot,* which seemed awfully small next to a sixty-foot sailboat. We looked at each other, and that was the most wonderful gift for me. We exchanged only a few fleeting words.

"Everything all right?" he shouted across the waves.

"Sure!" I yelled back, grinning at the sight of him.

All at once, I felt very near the European coast, as though I had almost arrived. But Roland stayed only a few minutes; all too soon, we were saying good-bye. He would be in some snug harbor by the following day and I would still be at sea. I was sad watching him sail away, wondering if I should have gone aboard his boat. Temptation had thumbed its nose at me, heckled me. But what if Neptune had meant to give me a ticket to safety by going ashore with Roland? Would the god of the sea now be angry with me for refusing this chance? While ridiculous, these questions did run through my mind. Fortunately, I still didn't know then that — contrary to what Roland had predicted — it wouldn't take me a "few days" to make a landfall; *it was going to take me a full seventeen days.* This was my one-hundredth day at sea and things just weren't going to get better.

It was mid-September and I was a full month behind schedule. The cold kept me from sleeping; and my fears of that next big storm never left me for a second. I realized that time was rushing by and that being at sea in such a small boat in the autumn would be suicide for me. Life aboard *Pilot* was becoming more and more difficult. I had no more changes of clothing, no soap for washing, no batteries for my GPS. And I was afraid my gas stove was going to malfunction. I also had to switch over to my reserve Argos radio beacon, since the battery had died on the main one. Everything was completely sodden in the cabin and, exposed to water constantly, my skin began giving me a lot of trouble. Arriving at the finish line was no longer a regular fantasy; in fact, I no longer dared believe in it, seriously doubting it even existed. I'd simply begun to doubt that my adventure would ever end. Right from Day One I had of course thought about reaching that finish line, imagining it a hundred times. But, maddeningly, easterly winds blowing from Europe kept shoving me back in my tracks. Those easterly winds were torturing me, making *Pilot* go backward. I rowed all day and, at night, but the wind pushed me back. For more than a month I'd been stagnating like this; I would make a little headway only to be blown back in my tracks. At times, I lost, in the space of twenty-four hours, what I had worked so hard to gain in more than four or five days. I hated being so helpless. What was more aggravating, the entire time I was struggling with this anticyclone, the weather in France was incredibly beautiful and warm. When I was getting nowhere fast and losing my marbles, I would start rowing regardless of the time, whenever the wind dropped off. At 3 A.M., I was in that cockpit — it didn't matter if it was hot — rowing and rowing. The meteorological picture changed constantly; each time the weather bureau forecast an improvement in conditions I believed them. And every time the east wind started blowing again, I was devastated. The prospect of facing one setback after another depressed me. Even my calendar, on which I crossed off the days, finished with the month of August. I'd have to tack on an extra page — a kind of supplement — and add groups of ten or fifteen days. Only there was no room for more calendar pages on the cabin bulkhead.

When the wind was too strong to struggle against, I set out my sea anchor. Then *Pilot*'s motion became really violent. She turned into a wild beast held by the tail, lashing out in every direction, trying desperately to free herself. Blows rained on my exhausted body, over and over. I spent entire days stuck inside the cabin, waiting for the weather to improve, for the wind to shift at last. I lived in austerity. I recalled the theories of the stoics, which I had studied for so long; I had admired Marcus Aurelius. But his kind of asceticism wasn't easy to practice. I tried to stay calm; I had to make up for the weaknesses of my body with the strength of my will. It wasn't quite that simple. I had heard about an ocean rower who'd gone mad in a situation like mine, right on the eve of his arrival. I tried to convince myself that it was just a rumor. On land, people were begging me to give up. My sailor friends — people who knew the sea at this time of the year — wanted to come out and get me. Then I had to convince them that everything was all right, that I was being careful and that, if a hurricane were forecast, I would reconsider my decision. The idea was unthinkable — giving up because I couldn't manage my stress or anxiety. For the time being, such an idea was out of the question. I would dig in my heels and take control. Which was exactly what I tried to do. In my first effort in this direction, I forced myself to dive into the water. I was going to clean off the hull of my boat.

The hull of *Pilot* had become seriously overgrown with barnacles. The anti-fouling paint intended to protect the boat below the waterline didn't last forever and this crossing had never been meant to take so long. But I could tell that her hull just wasn't sliding through the water the way it should have, and my oar strokes were consequently 50 percent less efficient. There was only one solution: clean her off. The water under me was over thirteen thousand feet deep, a genuine abyss. In the past few days, I had sighted sharks. First, I saw their tails and fins cutting through the water as they rapidly came barreling at me. Instinctively, I clutched the handrail — not exactly the time to fall in — as the powerful black shapes of the predators approached. Measuring between twelve and fifteen feet in length, they looked positively huge alongside my boat. Then, when they drew very close, they dove under me in one sinewy movement. I could have reached down and touched them. Their mass grazed the hull, making it vibrate beneath my feet. Reappearing on the other side, they began circling the boat aggressively, their round eyes gleaming and icy, reflecting a mixture of strength and confidence. Braced for action in the cockpit, I pulled one oar out of the rowlock, ready to defend myself. Watching their slightest movements, I waited. Not knowing how to attack the boat, the sharks tried one last method of intimidation: They lifted their heads toward me. Then the monsters disappeared as suddenly as they'd come. I expected to see them reappear, but the minutes went by and they didn't return.

On this particular morning, besides my rather off-putting shark memories, the water was icy. I might lack the strength to climb back aboard. But I had to clean *Pilot*'s barnacle-encrusted hull. I stripped off all my clothes and donned my harness so that I remained attached to *Pilot*. I'd never taken so long to get into the water — and I had always loved swimming. First of all, I was frozen stiff and, second, I wasn't at all sure I wanted to go through with the cleaning job. Who in their right mind really wanted to go sliding down into a pit full of sharks? My heart pounding, I took a lot of deep breaths. I had already phoned my family to let them know what I was doing. Marc had picked up the receiver. I knew that he would be waiting anxiously until I called him back, so I tried to work fast. After splashing myself as much as possible, I took the plunge. The frigid shock hit me from head to foot, taking my breath away, robbing my limbs of all feeling. I had to hurry. Working rapidly with my bare hands, I tore off the barnacles covering the hull while glancing over my shoulder to see if any sharks were coming. For the moment, none were near. The barnacles slid through my fingers and went spinning down in the abyss — the immense black hole —

beneath me. I continued to kick the water frantically, trying to make sure my feet stayed on the surface. *Come on, Maud, move it!* Now I needed to swim around to the starboard side. Only my lifeline was ten feet too short — I'd have to climb into the boat again and jump back into the water from the other side. No, I told myself, this couldn't be happening. But it was. And, since by this time I had almost no strength left and was freezing, it took great effort to pull myself up. Going back in the water was pure torture and I worked as fast as I could. When, totally exhausted, I climbed out of the water, I saw blood all over the cockpit and realized I'd somehow gashed my finger on a shell. Though shaking uncontrollably with the cold, I felt immensely proud, which provided an incredible shot of adrenaline. Even before drying myself off, I phoned Marc to reassure him. I only stayed on for a second but I knew how happy it made him. "Hurry up and get home," he said. I was in a hurry to see them. I missed my family terribly. After warming up with the one half-dry towel I still had left, I got dressed again and put on some water so I could eat something hot. I didn't want to take a chance on getting pneumonia.

Thirty minutes later, I could resume rowing. I picked up my oars and began pulling. The headwinds had dropped off and I prayed that it would stay that way.

9

Storm Warning — One Sparrow, Three Butterflies — Heading for Spain — Last Night Aboard

*T*HE MONTH OF SEPTEMBER HAD GONE BY. Now it was October and still no landfall. The easterly winds that blew against me relentlessly were torture. I knew the European coast lay only a few days away, yet it was eluding me because of the headwinds.

If I'd needed proof that fate was mocking me and that I was near land, a tiny sparrow, completely exhausted, alighted on *Pilot*. The scene was surrealistic: I was alone on the ocean, prey to strong winds from land, which made me lose a bit more mileage every day, dooming me to endless rowing. I was dreading the onset of another storm, becoming more and more likely as the year dragged on. And then one day, while already a bit giddy with the pleasure of speaking on the phone with my friend Thomas, in flew this small chocolate-colored bird. Trembling, it nestled in the fleece jacket I'd converted into a pillow. How strange that such a winged creature had lost its way, landing on a boat many miles out at sea. It must have been carried offshore by those same easterlies from Europe that were giving me so much trouble. I hastily said good-bye to Thomas and, motionless, began watching the bird. Tired, it paid no attention to me at all, simply taking a bit of a rest. A few minutes went by and then it got ready to depart. I bent down to help it find its way out of the hatch and then off it went.

The whole incident left me puzzled: What had prompted this sparrow to take off again when it had finally found shelter? I went on pondering this question for some time. Finally, I told myself that it couldn't have done otherwise. Something stronger than its weariness had compelled it to alight on my boat. It was something stronger than the hundred or so miles that separated it from land. It was its natural instinct as a bird. And what about me — exactly what made me tick? What made me go on rowing?

That same week, I had another unexpected visit: three yellow and gold butterflies carried to sea by the same easterly wind that flew over my boat. These tiny spots of color against the gray-blue sea were magical. I was fascinated by their natural splendor on an otherwise troubling morning. Three days earlier the news had been confirmed: An extremely severe storm was headed into my area. They were forecasting waves twenty-four- to thirty-feet high and gusts of fifty to sixty knots. I felt an oppressive weight on my chest.

"How long is it going to last?" I asked my weatherman on the cell phone rather insistently.

"It should take about twelve hours for the front to go through." In a lower voice, reassuringly, he added, "At the absolute maximum."

"What? *Twelve hours?* Impossible. I could never go through that again."

The weather report left me in an abysmal mood and I ended the call stunned. It would have been pointless to display my fear to him since there was nothing he could do. The more he knew that I was scared, the more reluctant he'd be to tell me the truth. And I wanted to know what was coming, even though there was nothing much I could do about it. But I did need to prepare myself psychologically and my boat physically. Even now I remember the keen disappointment I felt. What could I do? Unfortunately, the grim prospect of new hardship and suffering wasn't the only problem. There was also the fact that the coast was getting mighty close. Normally, without a storm warning, this proximity would have been good news. But within three days I might be battling a gale — and the threat of being driven ashore on some rocky stretch of coast was real. Storms in the Bay of Biscay are formidable, as every mariner knows. None of us will forget the distressing images at the start of the 2001 Route du Rhum when the sea wreaked absolute havoc. I didn't want to imagine my little *Pilot* in shallow seas so near land. The only solution was to rig up my sea anchor to check the boat's drift. I wouldn't row at all and wait for the storm to go through. This was the ultimate torture: slowing down when I was bursting with impatience to move ahead. It seemed nonsensical. Yet there was no other answer. I decided to keep plugging toward land — that is, until reaching the boundary I had set. Beyond that point, I'd be dangerously close to the rocky coast. I started praying that the weather report was wrong again —

but wrong in my favor, for once. I prayed that the depression would end its movement in my direction.

I didn't have long to wait for an answer. At dawn the following morning, my cellular phone rang. It was Pierre Lasnier, my meteorologist. There was such enthusiasm in his "good morning" that I knew he had some pleasant news for me.

"Listen, Maud, the depression is going through more to the north. You've had an incredible stroke of good luck — you're only going to get the edge of it. Hurry up and get a move on."

He blurted this out all in one breath, like a secret he couldn't have kept another second, bubbling over, as happy as I was. Ah, the relief of it all! How light, how young I felt. Only then did I realize just how tense I'd been for the past three days. My shoulders relaxed, my lungs filled with air again. "The storm's moving through more to the north!" I felt like setting it to music, shouting it from the rooftops. I was bursting with new energy. Yes indeed, it was going to be a great day.

Nevertheless, I had to reach the European coast very quickly. The plan calling for a landfall in France had been dropped. I was now steering for Spain, which wasn't as far away. It was a race against the clock. I had to make land before the winds shifted again and pushed me back offshore. So I went two days straight without sleeping, rowing most of the time. Ashore, my folks were in a tailspin. They had to arrange everything for my arrival in Spain. Marc and Yann were already on the highway, towing the trailer for *Pilot* behind their car. While I was pulling on my oars, they were driving toward Galicia, Spain's jutting northwestern corner. This trip wasn't over by any means. After forty-eight hours spent almost continually at the oars, I took a breather. Exhausted, I fell asleep in seconds. An hour went by before I groggily awoke: My feet were unusually wet. No, not again! Something must be wrong — where was the water coming from? I jumped up, pulled my mattress aside and saw . . . a leak. It was the ring-bolt on the stern. The rope for the sea anchor, which went through it, must have pulled it out. The sea was rough and the aft end of the boat was constantly awash — water was getting in back there. I had visions of the boat sinking. No, not this near the finish line! I felt sickened, panic-stricken. To think some people were already telling me I'd made it! The weather was too severe for me to go topside and inspect the damage, too dangerous to attempt any kind of repairs. It was October 5 and I still had no idea when I was going to complete my crossing. Monitoring this leak right up to the last day was going to be a real problem. I was worried, hoping it wouldn't get worse, shuddering at the thought of *Pilot* sinking a few nautical miles from the coast of Europe. When I tried to go back to sleep, I couldn't — every five minutes I started groping around the spot under my bunk where the water was coming in.

As evening fell, my radar detector beeped constantly. I hastily slid my oars out. It was impossible to get any sleep when danger was coming from everywhere. Right in the track of the freighters and container ships, the most heavily traveled shipping lane between the tip of France's Britanny Peninsula and Spain's Cabo Fisterra, I was like a squirrel in the middle of a highway. It was pitch-dark, with not so much as a star in the sky, and I was surrounded by lots of small lights — some of them white, some red and green. I could hear the fearful throb of powerful engines, coming from the left and the right. What should I do? Despite all my determination, I felt utterly helpless in the face of the problem. The right decision? That was anyone's guess.

I'd walked into a kind of trap. I decided to keep rowing as fast as possible to escape the risk of being run down. I absolutely had to get across the shipping lanes. I kept my eyes shut and held my breath. At times, the lights faded on the horizon; the ships were moving away from me. But minutes later, along came another one bearing down on me. Was there no end to this? Time dragged on. The interminable night made me desperate to see the dawn. I wanted to be done with it, to reach the finish at last. I thought back to everything that had happened since June 13 — and yet the final hurdle might involve being run down by a freighter. Not this close to the end! I tried to look at the upside: The chances of being rammed by a merchant ship were slim. The constant beeping of the radar jangled my nerves, and I rowed with my neck craned so I could see what was coming. I knew I had to get out of this. I'd sleep later. But there were times when my head drooped and hit the oars. I couldn't wait for a chance to rest, for this voyage to end.

When I glimpsed the first light of day, I began to feel better. There wasn't a single freighter anywhere. I checked my position on the chart one more time. I had to be close enough to land that I should already be seeing it. This was no time to slacken, so I rowed harder and harder. I became a robot with only one thought in my head: getting into La Coruña. The sea was rough, and *Pilot* was yawing and rolling; I had to use my feet to brace myself. From time to time, I lifted my eyes to the horizon — just in case some miracle might happen. And it was then, around 8 A.M., that, as if by magic, a very large dark cloud parted and I glimpsed it.

LAND! It was so beautiful. My heart racing, pounding, I felt charged with new energy; even my eyes stopped burning. In a flash, I forgot the night of terror I'd just lived through. Wildly excited, I phoned my shore team to give them the great news. They, in turn, would inform my Internet friends of my approaching, since I wanted to reassure all of them, too. Marc and Yann were nearing Galicia in the car, while friends from the Spanish Rotary Club were busy finding a boat sturdy enough to come out and meet me. According to the plan, they would all escort me into the port of La Coruña. I started rowing with all my might. I couldn't wait to pick up that first scent of land. How I longed to see greenery, trees, rocks. The closer I got, the more I realized (by twisting my head around) that the Galician landscape somehow resembled my own Brittany coast. But those steep cliffs lining the shore had me worried. Exactly how would I be able to land? Well, I supposed my shore team would have had time to figure that one out.

Toward noon, my team informed me they had a boat and would be coming out to join me. It was almost too good to be true. And that would be that; I would have completed the transatlantic crossing. Nevertheless, I refused to let down my guard. It was essential that I remain focused. "Be careful, Maud," a little voice seemed to whisper. "Often it's just when you think you've won that accidents happen. Watch out."

"We'll bring you a tuna-fish salad sandwich, Maud. Is that what you'd like?"

My mouth watered at the thought of savoring forgotten foods, say, for instance, a leaf of lettuce, a slice of tomato. . . . I waited, watching. They were on their way.

"We're on a big blue and white launch. We should be with you in ten minutes."

It was as though I was dreaming again. I had waited so long to hear those words. I'd waited 117 days, in fact. They were coming out for me at last and I'd soon be able to sleep. I couldn't sit still. I dove into the cabin for my binoculars, and then began studying the coast.

I saw them! I felt like jumping for joy. My father and brother were on their way out. It was no dream — they were coming. I wanted to laugh but couldn't. I hoped I hadn't changed too much, and that they could still recognize me. I hadn't slept in two days, my watch coat was encrusted with salt, and my hair was matted, filthy. The sun was shining, but a long swell was running; the seas must have been six feet high and I had to cling to the forward handrail. That was all I needed just then — falling overboard.

Their blue and white launch was by this time very close. As they passed me, I saw their faces. It was as though I'd never left. They hadn't changed one iota. Like me, they were smiling. Life was beautiful. I felt good, so very good.

And then came disaster. Things weren't as easy as I'd hoped. Their boat started circling me and, oddly, didn't come alongside. We talked over the radio. The skipper of their launch meant to keep his distance. He thought the seas were too dangerous for us to close the gap. Totally devastated, I was wondering, "Hey, guys, what's the story? Where's that tuna-fish salad sandwich?" No, were they really going away —

just like that? They'd actually leave me at the rocky cliffs of Galicia?

Minutes later, they announced they would indeed have to leave me. They needed to talk to the skipper of some other boat into bringing them back out. I was completely exhausted; with astonishing suddenness, the cumulative fatigue landed in my shoulder muscles. My skin started burning again. My so-called reception committee didn't even allow me the time to bemoan my fate. They just took off, their engine droning. And there I was — alone again. I was incredulous. Would I ever set foot on land? *Pilot* seemed as disconcerted I was, lurching and rolling. Worn out by her motion, I dropped onto my mattress and had a quick bite to get my strength back. Even the powdered, freeze-dried food I hoped I'd never need again seemed to heckle me. "See? Don't count your chickens before they've hatched," the bags of food sneered. Once again, my radar detector went off. I couldn't take much more of this — there was simply no let-up. I crawled topside again where the oars awaited me. With my backside sore from sitting, I couldn't stand that disgusting seat anymore; there was absolutely no way I could get comfortable on it. To top it off, salt managed to get everywhere and became excruciating wherever clothes chafed my skin.

The afternoon went by slowly and then night came. Apparently, my family still hadn't found the right boat, according to our frequent phone conversations. I was going to have to spend another horrendous night alone on my boat, making it three consecutive nights with next to no sleep. By now on the fishing grounds, I was surrounded by large trawlers. I would have given anything for some rest, for the strain to end at last; I desperately needed sleep. My eyes burned as I sat at the rowing station in the cockpit. The night was totally dark — not a glimmer of light, not a star, and I couldn't see the moon, either. I thought of only one thing: "Let that sun come up, please." I kept nodding over my oars, no strength left in my arms. My oars, my head, my body — everything seemed to get heavier and heavier. I saw the lights of boats in the distance; I saw one light after another. I wanted to yell over to them to leave me alone, to keep far away from me, to stop tormenting me. The place was crawling with boats. In the cold, I had to continue on my way. As the wind rose, I would have preferred being shut up below. I almost longed for the days when I was alone in mid-ocean and didn't have to worry about being driven against any coast. But here I was dozing off as I rowed only a stone's throw from rocks, unable to claw offshore. The seas were building up and becoming dangerous. There was something perverse about being so close to land and, yet, so alone. That afternoon I had relaxed my guard when my family came near, and now, returning to solitude was the ultimate letdown. I was concentrating on staying awake when, all at once, I saw a boat's large white light coming my way. I took a better look, hoping that my eyes had deceived me. I sat bolt upright. Since the boat was approaching a mile a minute, I shook off my sleepiness, my eyes trained on that monstrous spot of light tearing through the night. Then her bright light was directly abeam, bearing down on my hull at a right angle. I was terrified, grabbing for flares, foghorn, and flashlight. My heart started pounding like a jackhammer. What could I do? My legs were trembling and I felt somewhat faint, barely catching the handrail in time to keep from falling in, as *Pilot* bounced around. The oncoming boat rapidly closing the gap, I waved my light frantically. With the other hand, I activated the gas-operated foghorn that instantly produced an infernal racket. What did it matter if it deafened me? At least I'd be alive. In my panic, I began shrieking. I didn't want to be run down, certainly not here, so near the finish. But what could I do — jump into the water? Get off my boat? And if I did — then what? I would have no way of calling for help. The water was so cold I wouldn't last long, a few minutes at most. It didn't matter that I usually could think fast — I came up with no answer this time. All my hatches were battened down so that my boat could survive in case of a capsize. Now I had to choose: row like hell or shoot off flares. But I couldn't do both at once. The veins in my temples were pulsating. I had no way of telling how long this went on because time seemed to stand still. A bulldozer was coming and had its three huge searchlights trained on me, and yet, they couldn't see me.

"Stop!" I screamed.

At the last split second, I saw the captain come running from his cabin. The wake of his boat was already rocking *Pilot*. Seizing the wheel, he spun it, and his boat swerved away instantly.

He shouted a sentence in Spanish that probably meant something like, "What the hell are you doing out here?"

I yelled back in English, "Please try to watch where you're going!" But by now it no longer mattered, it was all history. He was gone, the threat of death had been removed. I was so tense I had muscle cramps. And, clinging so tightly to the handrail moments before, I'd managed to injure my hand without realizing it. In tears, I felt totally drained. The pressure was off, those lights on his boat were already losing their brilliance, disappearing as quickly as they'd come. But it astonished me that he hadn't even stopped to find out what I was doing there, to find out if I needed help. Well, anyway, it spared me the trouble of having to explain the inexplicable one more time. I phoned the shore to tell them what had happened.

"You'd better get out here. What with these rocky cliffs, the trawlers and the sea that's starting to build up, I'm not going to last very long."

I slumped down and, for a few minutes, sat huddled on the cockpit floorboards. I was extremely cold — probably the result of fatigue. Just let the sun come up, please! Without seeing me, trawlers kept circling me in the dark. The light atop my jackstay was still flashing, but it wasn't really bright enough to warn them of my location. Every hour, I got Marc on the phone to give him my position. Family and friends were desperate to come up with a solution. They weren't able to sleep, either, chasing around for a boat to charter, trying every possibility, every connection. Jean-François Copé, as mayor of the town where I lived and where I'd been born, asked the French minister of foreign affairs to contact his Spanish counterpart to have a naval vessel monitor my area. It was about 11 P.M. and I'd been in the dark for at least four hours. As boats kept moving around me my radar detector didn't stop beeping for a minute. My phone rang: Spanish sailors were calling. They were out there looking for me but were unable to see me. I repeated my position. The knowledge that they were approaching sufficed to bring my breathing rate back down to normal again. About an hour later, the Spanish navy reached me — a very large vessel painted battleship gray. I saw tiny men bundled up in thick watch coats on her bridge. I waved enthusiastically. Then they trained a huge searchlight on me, blinding me, but what a relief! I gave them a big grin. *Please don't go away like my first welcoming committee!* The Spaniards finally switched off their searchlight. Marc phoned then to say that the warship should remain standing by until he and my brother could get out there in the morning. Just one more night at sea. I began rowing slowly and the naval vessel kept turning around me in narrow circles. Obviously, they dared not move too far away for fear of losing sight of me. In fact, they were a little too close for comfort and I was scared they might actually run me down. But after a couple of hours they began to widen their circles. Soon, with lights everywhere, I no longer knew where the Spanish navy vessel was. I contacted Yann, who informed me that they'd chartered a boat. They were on their way! I made him say it again. Yes, it was true — my father and brother were coming, but I feared some new problem would stop them from reaching me. What if I had just dreamed all of this?

"We'll be with you in an hour."

Quite near the rocky coast, I waited for my adventure to end. I kept signaling with my flashlight.

"Maud, I think I see you. Go ahead, do it again so we can tell if it's really you."

I swung my flashlight again.

"Yes, okay! We'll be there in a few minutes."

I saw a light coming straight at me. It must be them — it

was! They're here! The blood coursing through my veins seemed to fizz like Champagne bubbles. It was lovely: seeing my family again, returning to earth. I wasn't at all sure I would still know how to walk. Their chartered boat was now only a hundred feet away. Marc and Yann waved at me. I sat looking at them — they seemed terribly rushed as news photographers bustled about onboard.

Time didn't have the same importance for me as it did for them. I lighted a red flare to celebrate the victory that convinced me, once and for all, that the transatlantic crossing was at an end. The finish was quite different from what I had imagined, and God knows I'd certainly spent enough time imagining it. My spirits soared, and everything seemed just fine. I wasn't thinking about having managed to cross the North Atlantic in a rowboat, or that I'd become the first woman to do it. Instead, I was only concerned with the fact that I didn't need to worry about dying anymore, that there wouldn't be any next big storm, that my stomachaches were finally going to end, and that at last I was returning to the bosom of my family. An immense surge of happiness overtook me. I was bursting with eagerness to set foot on land. Suddenly, there was the chartered boat — coming at me too fast. The solidly built vessel rammed into my port side, jolting me out of my bliss. I felt a rush of adrenaline, and everybody started screaming: "*Stop! Reverse!*" But the man at the wheel must have been deaf or he didn't understand, because his bow crashed into me again, only this time even harder. Several men began trying to use their feet and hands to fend us off; I crawled forward to protect *Pilot* as the other boat sent another violent shock through my hull. I couldn't believe what was happening.

"Back off! Get away, for God's sake!" I tried to yell.

I closed my eyes for a second. I was just too tired to utter another word. These characters were going to turn my boat into pick-up sticks.

Then the chartered boat started behaving like any normal vessel. The skipper had been under the impression that he was supposed to take me aboard.

"No, no, I'm not getting off. *Pilot* and I will come into port together and that's that. I won't leave her out here by herself."

The danger past, I remained seated in the cockpit. The sky had cleared and there was actually a full moon. It was the kind of night I loved, peaceful and mysterious at the same time. I relaxed. How beautiful life is! The stars appeared one after another and I saw their reflections on the water. I savored the aromas of this last night onboard *Pilot,* these last moments of complicity with the god of the sea.

"Thank you," I whispered to Neptune before crossing the frontier into the world of the terrestrials. "Thank you for helping me get here."

Epilogue: Following Your Dream

J UST AFTER 4 A.M. on October 9, 2003 I set foot on land after four months at sea.

In a few seconds, all the old terrestrial habits returned to memory. The scents and sounds that I'd been expecting for months seemed as familiar as if I'd left the day before. The anguish I'd experienced earlier that night melted away, no more than a distant memory. It was dark and a few stars wandered through the sky, but now the bright lights of the city attracted my attention. We were in an outlying section of the port city of La Coruña but, despite the apparent stability of the ground, I was still rolling and pitching. Several times I came close to falling on my face. As I leaned against the crane that would lift *Pilot* from the water, I felt dizzy and totally dazed by this flood of sensations. So, was this what it was like to finish? It was all so strange I couldn't believe it was over.

Around me, a dozen people — TV news cameramen, photographers, sailors — stared curiously, not daring to approach. I felt like an extraterrestrial. What had they expected to find? They hesitated to ask me questions, seemingly afraid of disturbing me. Yet God knows how much I wanted to talk, to tell my story. I was drunk with pleasure. People busied themselves around me while I watched *Pilot* being removed gently from the water. Without thinking, I walked up to my boat, suspended from the crane in webbing slings.

"Watch out! Don't stand under the load!" a man shouted. I backed up, drops of saltwater from *Pilot's* hull running over my face. I never took my eyes off her as they lowered her onto the dock; I even moved forward again to hold her gunwale, so that she wouldn't tip over on one side. It was the same for *Pilot* — nobody was giving her time to breathe. In an hour, she was sitting in her little trailer, securely fastened. The car backed up and was hitched to the trailer. Then we were ready to roll. It felt as if it had all happened in a minute; I was being carried so fast from one event to another; next, there would be the official finish slated for Orly Airport. I was in a hurry to see the rest of my family and all my friends. I just took the time to check that everything was properly stowed in *Pilot's* cabin and then climbed into the backseat of the car. Only then did I realize how terribly weary I was. My legs ached, my ears were stuffed and buzzing. I listened to my father and brother giving the latest news about everybody back home; their voices, which seemed to merge, were soothing as a lullaby. While listening to them didn't put me to sleep, I went into a kind of trance, a somewhat dazed reverie.

My first meal: *churros* — fried, sugared dough — and hot chocolate. I couldn't get over the delightful taste of solid (and sweet) food. In the Spanish café, I had the feeling everything was moving around me; the brown and red floor tiles were undulating, the walls oscillating. In my pocket, the cell phone never stopped ringing. It was the media wanting live interviews. The questions, always the same, became blurred:

"Well, how about your first impressions?"

"What are your worst memories, your best ones?"

"What does it feel like — becoming the first woman in the world to have rowed across the North Atlantic?"

I tried to explain the strange feelings ticking through me. My arrival at the finish line was already far behind me. What counted most, for me, was the daily struggle, the battle that went on moment to moment on my voyage. I had savored my success, that victory over myself, each time I crossed off an additional day on my calendar, each time I managed to extract that last drop of energy necessary to keep from giving up. Curiously, of all my daydreams, chief among them was my arrival at the finish line. Having had those rose-tinted images had restored my courage. But now my mind was elsewhere; my thoughts had gone beyond the transatlantic crossing. I was thinking about all the things I would see with new eyes. I'd blazed the trail on that northern route and hoped that someday other women would dare to attempt it.

"Are you sick of the ocean?" one journalist asked me.

No, of course not. Right from day one, the god of the ocean had allowed me to pursue my goal; he gave me the chance to accomplish my plan. I always had the feeling we were conspirators. Now a strong bond united us. He helped me to grow, to harden myself; he tested my determination and strengthened it; he tested my perseverance, my endurance. He taught me to take my time, all that it took to get all the way across.

I spent the next eight hours in the car, crossing into France and going as far as Biarritz, where a hotel room awaited me. The phone kept me awake, as one reporter after another threw questions at me, thrusting me brutally into the fast-paced life of the terrestrial.

Yes, my reentry into the everyday atmosphere was fast and indifferent. Actually, I had no choice in the matter. They gave me a few hours to sleep in a nice, warm bed. However, being overexcited, I hardly slept. There was too much to see in my hotel room, too many details. My eyes busily roved over the trifles — of the design on the curtains to the bric-a-brac on the shelves; from the wallpaper to the picture frames. I was even fascinated by the marks the steam iron had left on my white sheets. Oh, and the shower! What happiness! And all the good things to smell . . . everything seemed extraordinary. Even today, I frequently still marvel at hundreds of little things that I never considered important before the voyage. Now I see everyday life as a perpetual gift.

Marc and Yann went on their way, pulling *Pilot* behind the car. As for me, I had to catch the first flight for Paris the next morning. At breakfast, the hotel sent me a pastry boat of strawberries and a glass of milk — something I'd been dreaming about. (Who ever said that girls were hard to please?) In the bathroom mirror, I examined my face and body. I was covered with bruises; my skin looked deteriorated; my knees bore dark-red scars. I had lost twenty-two pounds. Some of my muscles had deteriorated while others had developed. Although I really didn't recognize myself, I was very, very happy to be alive.

Eight o'clock in the morning, arrival at Orly. A reception committee awaited me amid great pomp and ceremony: Jean-François Copé, general councillor for my home province; Karine Claireaux, mayor of Saint-Pierre and Miquelon, who had flown over just to honor me; and, sitting up front, my mother, Chantal. She was radiant. She came toward me, with her arms out. Like me, she seemed to be walking on a cloud. Her embrace returned me to the tender cheeks, the lily-of-the-valley perfume I so fondly remembered. I wept for joy. This was the most beautiful moment of my arrival. Many cried as I was passed from one person to another, besieged by questions, bombarded with kisses, and dazzled by camera flashes. I took new strength from their smiles. It was this human warmth, this effervecense I had so missed. May I never forget that moment; may I always stay as natural and innocent as I was that morning.

The stampede went on all day long: press conferences, televised interviews, photo sessions. . . . No time to think over what had just ended. I ran from one place to another, tireless, energetic, and happy. But then, the next day, I suffered the consequences — the repercussions of fatigue. Because I'd hardly stood upright for four months, it was now impossible for me to walk. My joints and legs were so swollen and painful that I could hardly stay on my feet. Fearing I had phlebitis, my family and friends rushed me to the hospital for an examination; I had vitamin and iron deficiencies — nothing else.

"It's only fatigue, you must get some rest," the doctors told me.

It was true. I was drained. Before this I'd had only one goal: getting across the Atlantic. I had wrestled with the fear in the pit of my stomach and anguish that I would soon run out of food and water. Quite simply, I'd struggled with the dread of dying. Then the pressure had fallen away all at once. My will had ruled my body, and now it was all over. Those last few days — which had passed with no precise, fundamental aim — had disoriented me. I felt alone, though surrounded by hundreds of people. They were asking me to summarize in a few seconds everything that I had gone through for 117 days. I kept getting the same questions. Here I was, someone who by dint of harsh lessons had learned to take my time, and now I had to respond quickly, streamlining my story a bit more each time.

Everything seemed reversed. I was sleeping less than before and kept on waking up; my body stayed alert even when I slept deeply. The radar detector didn't seem to want to stop beeping in my ear and I would find myself sitting bolt upright in my bed every hour. The transatlantic crossing hadn't really ended. I still felt tied to *Pilot* and, at times, I really missed her. I continued to sleep all scrunched up, as I did when I used to try to wedge myself in my bunk. Often, I woke with a start, thinking I was still *there*. That would immediately release a flood of good — and very bad — memories. Fortunately, my dream-catcher talisman wasn't far; it came from a Native American tribe and had been given to me before my departure. It had swung, suspended over my head, for those 117 nights, earnestly performing its role. Even now, this charm "imprisons" bad dreams so the sun may "burn" them up just after dawn. And it carefully watches over good dreams, letting them drop back on me every night. I believe that this talisman works . . . because desires for new crossings, full of glorious skies and the songs of whales, are beginning to awaken in me.

Acknowledgments

*M*Y PARTNERS IN THIS ADVENTURE WERE THE FOLLOWING:

— *Financial Backers:* Pilot, Buro+, UTB, Office of the General Councillor of the Department of Seine and Marne, Ecorebat et Fontenoy Immobilier
— *Technical Consultants:* Marine Pool, Plastimo, French Rowing Federation, Mercator, MaxSea, TD Com, and CEREC
— *Media:* France Info, *Madame Figaro,* TV Breizh
  Special thanks to 47° Nord for their assistance throughout those 117 days.

For their patience and selflessness, I want to express my debt of gratitude to my land party, my godfather who was always there for me, my tireless Webmaster, my persevering communications agency, my audacious and foresighted partners, and all those — from Saint-Pierre and Miquelon, from France, Canada, Australia, and other regions of the world — who throughout this crossing, backed me, advised me, and encouraged me. I share this victory with all of you.

The editor wishes to thank Thomas Bez and Jean-Christophe L'Espagnol for their assistance in producing the photo section.